Psyc

Everything You Need to Know to Develop Your Psychic Abilities

John Simone

REVIEW COPY
NOT FOR SALE

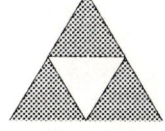

Three Pyramids Publishing

Psychic Awareness: Everything You Need to Know to Develop Your Psychic Abilities

Copyright © 1995 by John Simone. All rights reserved.

All rights reserved. No part of this book may be reproduced or transmitted in any form or by any means, electronic or mechanical, including photocopying, recording or by any information storage and retrieval system without written permission from the author, except by a newspaper or magazine reviewer who wants to quote brief passages in connection with a review.

Published by Three Pyramids Publishing
Editorial Offices: 201 Kenwood Meadows Drive, Raleigh, NC 27603-8314 USA

Manufactured in the United States of America

First Edition: October 1995

Library of Congress Catalog Card Number: 94-61607

ISBN 1-886289-03-4

Cover Design: Joseph S. Weintraub
Editor: Catherine Johnson

Dedication

Richard Vasconi is a loving, gentle, generous friend. Both of us realize that the enormous power of the cosmos brought us together again in this lifetime. We have shared many an adventure together, with many more to come, I hope. Rich is the kind of friend everybody wishes they had. This book would not have been completed without his encouragement.

Barbara Straub, the owner of Unicorn Books in New Milford, Connecticut, is another special friend. When I first began teaching metaphysical classes, Barb invited me to teach at Unicorn. The classes were well received and a new career opened up for me.

Georgiana Byrne piqued my interest again in metaphysical topics after years of focusing on other things. "Gi" and I rediscovered Glastonbury, England, my favorite place on earth, and she introduced me to a new career - writing about metaphysical subjects, and to another wonderful teacher who had a profound influence on my own psychic development, *Craig Junjulas*.

And to all the students of my Psychic Awareness (and other) classes - a special thank you!

About the Author

John Simone is an internationally-known professional psychic and trance channeler. He lectures and conducts workshops on various new age topics. He lives in Raleigh, North Carolina, and frequently travels to Glastonbury, England, where he offers workshops and trance channelling sessions. He is currently writing a book called *Intuitive Tarot*.

Psychic Awareness is the textbook for John Simone's Psychic Awarness class which has been held at Ulster County Community College, Stone Ridge, New York, and at Wake Community Technical College, Raleigh, North Carolina.

Books from Three Pyramids Publishing are available at special discounts for bulk purchases, sales promotions, fund raising, or educational purposes. Special editions can be created to specifications. For details contact: Special Sales Department, Three Pyramids Publishing, 201 Kenwood Meadows Drive, Raleigh, NC 27603-8314 USA.

Contents

Chapter 1 - Introduction 1

Chapter 2 - Getting Started 5
   Arrangement of Topics 5
   Exercises 6
   Keeping Journals 8
   The Group Approach or Self Study? 9
   If you have questions 11

Chapter 3 - The Basics 13
   What is Metaphysics? 14
   Preliminary Steps for All Psychic Work 15
   Breathing Exercise 17

Chapter 4 - Relaxation 19
   Relaxation Techniques 20
   Relaxation Exercise 23

Chapter 5 - Creative Visualization 25
   Creative Visualization Exercise - The Meadow 28

Chapter 6 - Meditation 31
   Meditation Visualization Exercise 33

Chapter 7 - Energy 37
   Manipulating Your Energy 39
   Developing Receptivity 40
   Telepathy Exercise 41

Chapter 8 - The Aura 43
- Learning to See the Aura 51
- Seeing the Aura 54
- Aura Readings 55
- Protection 58
- Astral Travel 60
  - Conscious Astral Travel Exercise 61
  - Astral Travel in Dreams Exercise 63
- Working on the Astral Plane 64
- Thoughtforms 65
  - Creating a Thoughtform Exercise 66
  - Care and Feeding of Thoughtforms 68
  - If Your Thoughtform Does Not Work 69

Chapter 9 - Karma 71

Chapter 10 - Reincarnation and Past Life Regression ... 77
- Soul Groups 80
- Spiritual Guides 81
- Past Lives 83
  - Past Life Regression Exercise 84
- Techniques for Past Life Regression 86
  - Regressing to a Significant Past Life Exercise 92
  - Scanning A Past Life for Details 94
  - Considerations for Past Life Regressions 95

Chapter 11 - Healing 97
- Methods for Psychic Healing 100
- Using Healing Energy 101

Chapter 12 - Working With Color 107
- Color Energies and Chakras 108
- Working with Color and Energy 110
- Energizing the Aura with Color 113
- Color for the Imagination Impaired 113
  - Color Exercise 114

Chapter 13 - Psychic Readings 115
   Receiving a Psychic Reading 115
   Performing a Psychic Reading 120
   Methods for Receiving Psychic Information 123
   How the Tools Work 128

Chapter 14 - Channelling 131
   How Channelling Works 133
      Channelling Exercise - Meeting Your Guide 134

Chapter 15 - Crystals 137
   Crystal Attunement Exercise 139
   Working With Crystals 140
   Elementals 143
      Crystal Visualization Exercise 144
   Crystals and Chakras 146

Chapter 16 - Ethics 149
   Ethics for Psychic Healing 154

Index 157

1

Introduction

That this book is named *Psychic Awareness* is no accident. Those who are not aware of the world around them cannot be psychic, and conversely, those who are psychic must, by definition, be more aware than others.

Psychic development is a process by which you will increase your sensitivity to all of the world around you. Becoming psychically receptive is only part of the developmental process. During the next few weeks, as you study the topics presented in this book, you will find yourself becoming more self-aware. As a result, the world around you will appear to have changed. Take a moment now to meditate on your life, your goals, and the reasons why you want to study psychic development at this time. After several months of study, reflect back and examine the ways in which your life has changed. Nearly everyone who does this mental exercise finds enormous differences between the way they were when they started to study psychic development topics and the way they are after studying these topics. It is a gentle process, but an effective one.

As you grow in awareness, you will become more sensitive to both your physical world and to other planes of existence. You might see the energy of life in a different way. As you continue to study and grow, parts of your everyday life that now seem exhausting and difficult will become joyful and less complicated. As you begin to truly understand how life works, it becomes easier to change the things in your life that no longer work for you or that you no longer want. Instead, you will be empowered to find new ways of looking at and dealing with life.

I urge you to apply to your own life the information you gain by reading this book, by taking classses, or by whatever method you choose to learn and grow. To understand others, you must first understand yourself. You are your own workshop and you must first understand and apply your theories to your own life before they can become valid for others. And remember: what is valid for you is not necessarily applicable for anyone else. You might also notice that your opinion of what is valid metaphysically changes constantly.

It is always a good idea to take careful notes. I use various notebooks and journals to record information that I have gained. You might be excited now about your success in using a specific crystal in a past life regression, but five years from now, it is going to be difficult to remember which crystal you used, if you have not done any past life regressions using it in the intervening years!

I, as a teacher, cannot make you aware. My best effort will be to keep you awake and interested. You cannot become psychic by being near other psychic people, and you cannot become more aware just by attending a class or reading a book. This is a gentle but effective process of *self-development* requiring effort, patience, and practice. Each technique that is illustrated is designed to make you more aware of some aspect of living on the planet and in the cosmos, and to perhaps give you an experience that you have never had before. Each topic builds on what has been learned earlier, and there is a method behind the way topics are arranged. For that reason, I urge you to tackle the topics in the order in which they are presented.

You can learn something from me. But you will learn much more from your higher self, your inner self, your guides, and your guardian angels. My intent is to show you how to contact those sources of wisdom, love, and power. Those are the resources you will have to fall back on when you need them!

If your intent is honorable, you will be supported by the higher realms in all you do. My intent is to show you how you can change your life for the better. I know it works; I have done it for myself. Many of the techniques I will illustrate for you are hundreds or thousands of years old.

There is a question of ethics and responsibility in using these techniques. The chapter on ethics describes some of the concepts to consider as you determine your personal code of ethics. You can misuse these techniques, it is true; you can also get results using them. But if you attempt to control or harm others, the power to make changes is taken from you (or more likely, turns against you) by the universal law of cause and effect. I have seen it happen many times: those who try to manipulate or control others are not successful (for long). Try it if you like, but understand that when you do, the universe will return a strong lesson to you. I have never known it to fail.

If you have any questions about any developmental topic, or a technique, close your eyes and meditate. Use your own insight to answer your questions. *You* are your own best source. I want you to understand that you create your own reality; that you alone are responsible for your life; and that you alone have the power and ability to live joyfully. My philosophy about awareness is that this is **your** world. What you do with it is your own choice and nobody else's. If you have a happy and fulfilling life, it is because that's what you chose.

Also, remember to *release your expectations.* I hope you are not expecting these techniques to make you a psychic. That cannot be done, because you cannot absorb the ability to be psychic any more than you can be artistic by taking a class on drawing. I can show you how to exist in a way that is different from the way you exist right now. Because that way of life involves becoming more open and aware, you will automatically become more psychic. If you insist on holding on to that vision of what life *should* be, you will be disappointed. Those same expectations will hold you back from any kind of development in any area.

Welcome to Psychic Awareness!

2

Getting Started

Becoming more aware, both personally and psychically, is a process of understanding yourself: who and what you are, and how you fit into the world. That definition may change by the time you complete this book.

Arrangement of Topics

In any course of study, how the topics are presented is a major contribution to how well the concepts are understood. It is important to not only understand the basics, but also to be able to put them into practice before tackling more advanced concepts. In the study of metaphysics, this is especially important. Trying to manipulate subtle energy vibrations is dangerous if you are not fully aware of the effects that the vibration can produce in the physical world.

The first few topics presented are basic information about becoming more receptive. Other topics are introduced as the intricacies of energy manipulation are studied and assimilated.

Some of the topics described in the book allow you to work in a **receptive state** in which you receive information. Other topics allow you to work in a **projective state** in which you send energy out into the cosmos. The basics are the same in either case.

Exercises

In the course of studying a particular topic, it is helpful to see how the concept actually works. I have included exercises on various topics to help you familiarize yourself with the practical use of the topic.

Beginners in the metaphysical fields should follow the exercise exactly as it is presented the first few times it is used. Those individuals who have some previous exposure to the topic can use the exercise as presented or make minor changes to it. Significant changes, of course, negate the value of doing the exercise, since each exercise was created to illustrate specific concepts and to present them in a specific order.

In my *Psychic Awareness* classes, students have several advantages in their study of these topics. During creative visualizations, they can simply close their eyes and visualize because someone else is leading the visualization. If you use this book for self-study, you probably do not have the luxury of having someone else go through the visualizations with you. In this case, you need to use alternative methods to do the visualizations.

One good method is to tape record the visualization. Slowly read the visualization exercise from the book, allowing time where necessary so that impressions can be registered. It is useless to rush through a visualization, leaving no intervals to allow yourself to fully receive an impression.

Psychic energy is free flowing; you cannot force yourself to register what has not yet been received. When you play your recording of the visualization, you will want to have enough time to register and enjoy the impressions you receive. Remember, the exercises that involve creative visualizations are designed to illustrate, among other concepts, how enjoyable and loving life can be. It is rather like taking a tour of a beautiful, relaxing place. You cannot enjoy the serenity and peacefulness if your tour guide - in this case, your own voice - is urging you constantly to move on to the next stop of the tour.

Of course, if you want to work alone, you can memorize the visualizations.

For exercises like the past life regressions where you must respond to a question, it is helpful if you use two tape recorders. Record the visualization on one tape, remembering to allow time between questions so that you can respond. Play the visualization on one recorder and record your responses on the other. Because it records the original tape as you record your visualization, your second tape will have a complete regression on it that includes the questions asked on the original tape.

Paragraphs that begin with the tape recorder symbol 📼 can be read directly into a tape recorder. Before you start recording, read the entire exercise. Some exercises have comments that do not need to be recorded onto the tape. Leave a few moments of blank tape at the end of each section so that you will have enough time to provide a response or to register your impressions. It is always best to leave a few seconds more than you think you need.

These exercises are not designed to be tests of your abilities. When you take a test, your mind snaps into a very solid beta-wave brain state. This virtually ensures that you will not be able to receive information psychically. It is the most effective blocking tool of which I am aware.

A particular problem is seen in classes like my *Psychic Awareness* class. Although most students are not aware of it, their tendency is to remain in a strong beta-wave state because they are sitting in a classroom taking what is called a class. If you are an adult, you probably spent at least twelve or thirteen years in classes. Your mind is so conditioned to being tested scholastically that it automatically reverts back to an optimum state for taking tests. It is this conditioning that works against you.

You can overcome this problem. It requires changing the way you view your educational endeavors. Focus on getting as much as you can out of a class (or a book) and do not worry about what others are doing or how well they are doing. It has absolutely no correlation to how well you learn. The less involved you are with others, the more you can assimilate.

Keeping Journals

As you study the vast subject of metaphysics, it is helpful to keep a journal of what you have experienced. In working with creative visualizations or dreams you access a higher vibration, an energy that is difficult to integrate with the energy of the physical world. As such, the conscious mind has trouble recording its impressions because they are so different from daily life. You will find that much of what you have experienced is forgotten a day or two later. For this reason, it is useful to keep a journal in which you can record these fleeting impressions.

In the past, I have kept a dream journal and several

other journals on other topics. If you are going to record your impressions as you work, keep a separate journal for each topic. The energy of each topic is reflected in your journal when you write your impressions down. Record only dream impressions and interpretations in your dream journal; information about other topics (creative visualizations, for example) is not useful for interpreting dreams and might actually be more confusing than helpful.

The Group Approach or Self Study?

There are two methods that can be used in learning the material presented in this book. One is self-study, an independent program in which you tackle the topics on your own. The second method is group study. That, of course, is the method used in my *Psychic Awareness* classes and it has produced excellent results in the many years that I have been teaching it.

Both methods have inherent strengths and weaknesses which need to be weighed in your own circumstances as you decide between the two methods.

By studying alone, you will not have the distractions and time constraints that are part of the group study process. You can study when and where you like without having to depend on others to contribute. Much of my own training in the metaphysical fields was achieved through self-study. There is no pressure to keep up with the group, and there is no system for comparison with the abilities of others. You are free to learn at your own capacity and in your own way.

In group study, you have the opportunity to exchange ideas with others, and also to receive help from others if there is a topic that you do not understand. Group study can be enjoyable because there are others with whom you can share your experiences. The possibility always exists for gregarious people to dominate a group, leaving those more introverted folks to sit silently with unanswered questions.

Also, some exercises are oriented by their very nature to group activity - past life regression exercises are an example. Some of the exercises are more easily accomplished if they are led by a group facilitator. However, there is no exercise in this book that cannot be adapted to self-study.

Base your choice on what is comfortable for your situation. Use what works for you.

If you choose to study with a group, here are some guidelines that might help:

☆ Choose the members of the group carefully. Make sure that everyone has similar intentions in studying these topics.

☆ Release any expectations about what might happen. Allow the synergy (group energy) to manifest something that is useful for each of you.

☆ Provide sufficient time for the exercises. While the background material can be studied either during the group meeting or at other times, it is the exercises that provide the most growth. Try each of them several times, not just once.

☆ If a facilitator is used, allow different members to serve as facilitator. Some people respond well to certain types of voices or demeanor, while others do not respond as well. Switching the duty of facilitator among members of the group enables growth for all.

☆ There is no *right* or *wrong* in learning this topic. Each person learns and grows in their own way. Subscribe to the concept that each person's method is right for him or her, while allowing for a particular method to be inappropriate for you. If an exercise produces no effect, try it another way.

☆ The material in this book requires fourteen hours of study when I teach it to a group. Do not rush through it. The idea is not to learn the material as quickly as possible, but to learn it in the way that works best for you. You cannot put any of it to use if you merely skim over the topics.

☆ Practice the techniques with different people. There are many variables to consider when any two people do anything, so take this into account and optimize your study time. After all, you do not have to work with those in your study group forever.

If you have questions

Always use your inner knowledge if there are processes about which you have questions. Your higher self can access information on topics about which you have no prior knowledge. It is the best resource you have. Using your higher self wisdom is part of what studying metaphysics is all about. Doing whatever feels appropriate, as long as it is ethical, always works. Use this capability in all areas of your life. People who have so-called "charmed lives" are simply following the information given them by their higher selves. They live intuitively. You can too.

Whether you choose group or individual study, if you have any questions for which you cannot find an answer, you can write to me, in care of the publisher, and I will try to help.

I am also interested in receiving comments on topics, processes, or exercises in this book. They might be incorporated in future revisions.

If I use your comments in a future revision of the book, I will send you a free copy of the revised edition.

3

The Basics

At the beginning of the first session of the *Psychic Awareness* class, before doing anything else, I write the following on the blackboard:

$E=MC^2$

<u>MATTER</u>
Solid \
Liquid $\rangle$ Atoms $\rangle$ Electrons, Protons, Neutrons $\rangle$ Quanta
Gas   /

Many of the students begin to look around in confusion, checking their course descriptions with each other and asking if they are in the correct room. They assume that the scientific information on the blackboard has no relation to a class about psychic abilities.

I use the two concepts illustrated here to help explain what metaphysics is all about.

The first line describes Einstein's Special Theory of Relativity. It says that energy (E) is equal to mass or matter (M) accelerated to the speed of light (C) squared. That is, matter is only energy that exists in a state so dense that we can physically perceive it.

The second concept illustrates the theory of quantum physics. Basically, it states that all matter (solids, liquids, and gases) is composed of atoms, which are all composed of electrons, protons, and neutrons, which are all composed of quanta. A **quantum** is an individual packet of pure energy that can act as either a particle or a wave. Particles are matter; waves are energy, such as sound and light. This theory states that everything is composed of pure energy, and it is only its representation in the physical world that makes us perceive it as energy or as matter.

This explains how energy works. In addition to being able to work physically, humans can work energetically as well. This allows us to access all of the kingdoms, all of the energetic bodies, our higher selves, and the energy of the universe.

For many years, scientists have accepted the concept that the universe is composed of one basic material: pure energy. If you have trouble relating to some of the concepts of metaphysics, be aware that they all have counterparts in the physical world. There is an old metaphysical saying: as above, so below. Everything that is represented in the physical world has representations in the energy realms. Also, any concept that applies to the physical world can be applied to the metaphysical world.

What is Metaphysics?

Metaphysics is the branch of philosophy that seeks to explain the nature of being and reality. The literal meaning of the word metaphysics is "beyond physics." Grolier's Encyclopedia defines metaphysics this way: "Metaphysics is that area of philosophy which concerns itself with the nature and structure of reality. It deals with such questions as: Are the objects we perceive real or illusory? Does the external world exist apart from our consciousness of it? Is reality ultimately reducible to a single underlying substance? If so, is it essentially spiritual or material? Is the universe intelligible and orderly or incomprehensible and chaotic?"

Metaphysicians try to understand the connections of the universe. They understand that everything is connected to every other thing. As you acquire psychic skills, you are exploring the world of metaphysics.

Preliminary Steps for All Psychic Work

There are five basic concepts that must be discussed before you can begin working in the psychic realms:

☆ Breathing rhythmically

☆ Centering (aligning the chakras so that impressions from the solar plexus can be received)

☆ Grounding (releasing excess energy)

☆ Relaxation of the physical body

☆ Collecting energy

Breathing in a steady rhythm helps relax the body by increasing the flow of oxygen in the bloodstream. Take slow, deep breaths. It can be helpful to inhale through the nose and exhale through the mouth, because changing from the way you breathe normally helps you focus on your breathing technique.

Centering is a process in which you settle your conscious mind in order to get an approximation of where your energy is and what condition it is in. Once you understand how "you" are at that given point in time, you can either increase your energy if you are feeling dissipated or decrease and compact it if you are feeling expansive and flighty. The point is to get your energy arranged neatly in your aura, regulating it to a great degree. When you finish, your aura will resemble an egg; it becomes relatively smooth and firm on the outside like an eggshell. If you can see it psychically, it will appear to be smooth and multi-colored like a soap bubble. Your chakras will also align themselves vertically into a straight line and move horizontally into place.

Grounding is a process in which you release excess energy into the ground (hence the name) or push it away into space, whichever one feels more comfortable to you. If you send your extra energy into the earth, remember to visualize it streaming directly down into the hot, molten center of the planet. There it will become transformed into pure universal energy and used by the earth itself in its regeneration processes.

Relaxing the muscles ensures that your energy can flow freely throughout the physical body. The process is described in the next section.

Collecting energy is a process in which you access universal energy and bring it into the aura. This is usually done using creative visualizations or meditation.

Breathing Exercise

As in any psychic work, remember to physically relax first by beginning breathing exercises.

📖 Breathe in, hold the breath, and breathe out. The idea is to take the automatic function of breathing and let the conscious mind occupy itself with it, so that it both frees up the unconscious mind to do other work and also keeps the conscious mind occupied. As you breathe out, let the tension of the day escape with the breath. As you perform this exercise, notice that you feel somewhat more solidly "inside" the body than usual. This is called **centering**.

📖 As you continue to breathe, first tighten all of your muscles, and then let them go limp. Visualize a warm, soothing violet colored liquid swirl about your feet. Bring that feeling of warmth up the legs, up the trunk, into the arms and hands and out through the fingertips, and into the shoulders, neck, and head. Now let the beautifully colored warm energy circulate in and through your body until you can feel it in every cell. Swirl it around your body and allow it to grow larger. It fills your astral body with wonderful violet light.

📖 When you are centered, you tend to be completely aware of your body and you can feel the energy that is you being completely contained in your physical body. As you continue to bring in energy, however, it tends to make you feel a bit "spaced out," meaning that you filled the space that you occupy with energy so completely that you need more room. You are literally "out of space" in which you can store your energy.

📖 Now open the crown chakra at the top of your head by visualizing small doors opening inward. White light (which appears visually as if it were sparkling clear water) pours in through the opened chakra and washes down through your entire body and exhausts out through your feet. Feel the last of your tensions being swept away into the very center of the earth and changed into positive energy. This is called **grounding**.

By grounding, you open a channel through which excess energy can exhaust. This removes that light-headed feeling and allows you to feel the energy flowing through your physical body rather than just moving around inside it.

You are now very relaxed. You are calm and relaxed. The violet energy is swirling around and through you, and you are very relaxed.

Picture yourself now in an outdoor place that is very special to you. If it exists in reality, go there in your mind. You can see it again. If you cannot easily picture such a place, then imagine one. It is a very beautiful and relaxing place. The sun shines overhead, a gentle breeze blows, and you can hear birds call to their mates in the distance. Hear, feel, smell - *be* in this place now.

4

Relaxation

Why must you relax? It is simple, really. Your physical body and your energetic body (called the **etheric** body) are intimately linked; your physical body reflects the condition of your etheric body. Normally, the etheric body automatically processes energy in the optimum way to keep you healthy and fit. If you feel dumpy or tired, it is because your etheric body is losing more energy than it is receiving. If you feel peppy it is because your etheric body has taken in more energy than your physical body needs.

If your physical body is tensed, as it is most of the time except when you are asleep, muscles are contracted. In a physical sense, when all those muscles are clamped down and pressing on your circulation system, it restricts the flow of blood. Blood carries oxygen, and the brain needs oxygen to function. Less blood flowing means less oxygen is being delivered to the brain and muscles, which means you have less mental and physical capacity.

That is a physical explanation; there is also a metaphysical one. It takes a lot of energy to contract those muscles, and that means there is less energy available to your etheric body. Your consciousness is not a physical function. Conscious thought does not occur in your brain. You think with your entire physical body, but more appropriately, conscious thought is processed by the etheric body. That is why you find it difficult to concentrate when you are tired.

Relaxation Techniques

Place your feet flat on the floor and sit erect but comfortably. Your hands should be on your lap, on the arms of your chair, or on a table. Uncross any limbs that are lying on or under other limbs. *Consciously* start at one end of the body and relax the muscles. Proceed to the other end of the body and make sure all of your muscles are relaxed by the time you get to the other end. I usually start at the feet, but you can start at the head if that feels more comfortable to you. The idea is to remember to start at one end and work your way to the other so that it is a logical, automatic process. If, for example, you start with the hands, then move to the thighs, then jump back to the neck, then the chest... well, there is a good chance that you would forget something and about halfway through the meditation you would begin to notice that forgotten area because it will feel so different from the rest of your body! Be methodical and it will pay off. After repeating this exercise a dozen or more times, muscular relaxation will become second nature.

And do not use this technique only when you are meditating! Five minutes of complete relaxation in the middle of the day will relax and renew you and make your day flow more smoothly. You can use this technique any time you feel stressed. You can do it at work or while waiting in traffic (if you want to use it while driving, be sure to pull off the road and stop first).

A more advanced relaxation technique that can be used once you learn to effectively relax physically involves first relaxing the muscles as usual. Imagine all tension draining from your body through the feet. Visualize a set of doors a bit above your head that open downward towards your skull. The place where you visualize them hanging in space above your head is the edge of your aura. You already know where that is. Allow pure, clean energy - frequently called **white light** - to flow down through the opened doors. This energy resembles pure clear water, not white paint. As it flows in through the opening, it washes through your aura and cleanses it. And, since your aura permeates the denser bodies, feel the energy cleansing your etheric and physical bodies too. As it pours in at the top it washes away tension and negativity and carries them away into the earth. Once you feel the energy in your aura (and you will feel a difference), breathe in to bring more energy into your physical body. As you breathe out, imagine more tension and negativity leaving your body on the air that you exhale. The process of letting energy in and flushing out negativity also has some physical benefits. Most people do not breathe deeply enough. Interestingly, it has been noted that many smokers can easily quit smoking when they learn to breathe as deeply in everyday life as they do when inhaling! Breathe deeply as often as possible, not only during meditation. The process becomes easy and automatic with practice.

Do not forget to close the doors above your head when you finish, or you will find yourself becoming flighty and ungrounded. Those open doors will also let the negativity that often surrounds other people to enter your aura. Remember also to visualize the negativity and tension that you release from your body being pushed far away, either into the center of the earth or far out into space. Do not let it dribble out and puddle around you in an unfocused way because you will just bring it back in.

Remember, I am talking about deep relaxation, not just a simple loosening of your surface muscles. Visualize your muscles relaxing right at their connection to the bones and all along their length. Do not forget to relax your eyelids and cheek muscles and unclench those teeth! There are a lot of tiny muscles in the face and releasing tension there is as important as releasing it in larger body areas. If there is any location on the body that is neglected when relaxing, it is facial muscles, probably because we spend so much time carefully arranging our faces to present our image of ourselves to everyone else.

There is another reason for relaxing. When you deliberately slow down your body processes by consciously relaxing, you will enter an **alpha-wave** brain state. Your normal conscious state is called the **beta-wave** state.

In the alpha state, your brain waves slow considerably and become highly rhythmic. When this happens, you have entered what is called an **altered state of consciousness**. While in the alpha state, you will be more psychically receptive. It is difficult, if not impossible, to receive psychic impressions in the beta state.

The reduction or elimination of stress in the alpha state is also physically beneficial. For example, your heart and pulse rates slow down, your blood pressure drops, and your body eliminates more toxins; blood vessels open slightly, you breathe more deeply, and the slower brain wave patterns make it easier to concentrate and to retain information.

The more you relax, the easier it becomes. Use it whenever you think of it during the day, and you will be happier and healthier!

Relaxation Exercise

Use this technique as an exercise to practice relaxation.

▣ Sit comfortably with head and body completely supported, or lie on a couch or bed or on the floor. Close your eyes, but keep your eyelids relaxed. Do not squint your eyes or clench your teeth.

▣ Inhale deeply and slowly through your nostrils. Hold your breath a few seconds, then exhale through the mouth. Concentrate on your breathing. As you exhale each breath, imagine the tension of the day escaping through your mouth with every breath.

▣ Inhale and hold your breath as you tighten every muscle in your body. Feel the compression in your muscles. Then exhale and let your muscles relax so that your body feels loose and limp like a rag doll.

▣ Now return to that rhythmic breathing. Breathe in through your nose, hold your breath a few seconds, and exhale through your mouth. Imagine warm, soothing energy surrounding your feet, as though they are soaking in warm water. Feel the muscles loosen and relax. Feel the blood flowing gently and smoothly up your legs as it carries this warming energy up your body.

▣ As the warmth travels up your legs, your trunk, your shoulders, and down into your arms and hands, remember the most peaceful place you have ever been. If you prefer, create a special dream place where there is beautiful scenery; an imaginary place where you control the events and have no cares or troubles.

▣ Be sure to involve all five physical senses and your entire thinking and feeling system in this scene. *Feel* the sun on your skin; *smell* the flowers; *hear* the birds chirping and the bees buzzing; *see* the mountains in the distance. If there is a stream or pond, *taste* the water. Let this feeling of peace and tranquility surround you and support you totally and safely as the energy now rises into your neck and your head.

▣ Inhale, imagining a golden-white light shining down from above your head. Let this soothing light energy pour into the top of your head as if the spiritual energy in your aura were pouring in like a gentle waterfall. Let it cascade down through your body bringing light and love into your total being.

▣ As you exhale, allow this refreshing energy to push all the remaining tension out of your hands and feet into the chair or bed. Visualize the tension as dark, heavy energy patterns, and watch it flow from your body, through the chair or bed, through the floor and into the earth.

▣ Silently ask your body to release the tension it holds. Feel and enjoy the sensation of the refreshing energy flowing through your body and your aura. Allow yourself to feel the sensation of total relaxation within the protective bubble of your whole aura by visualizing yourself inside a ball of radiant light, feeling peaceful and tranquil.

▣ Expand your mind's energy until it completely fills the aura, and imagine that you are a radiant ball of consciousness.

▣ To end this relaxation session, take a very deep breath and silently say, "I am calm and relaxed."

You can use this statement as a triggering mechanism for returning to this state of deep relaxation at another time.

5

Creative Visualization

One of the techniques used often in metaphysics is called **creative visualization**. This is nothing more than using what you know as your imagination to create a new reality. There is enormous power in the mind. We can tap this power easily, but unfortunately, we often use it to program our reality in a negative way. We use the power of the mind to set limits on what we can achieve. Children are often told, "you can't do that" and, sooner or later, they begin to believe it. When the child becomes an adult, that belief is still lurking in the area of the mind known as the subconscious, and it will still have a limiting effect on that person's reality.

Creative visualization in its most basic form seems to be nothing more than an exercise in imagination. But it is far more than that. On the astral plane, your dreams are your reality in the same way as the physical world is your reality now. What you imagine is real. Whatever you visualize, if given enough energy, becomes real. If you need more money, for example, visualizing an abundance of money makes it reality in the astral plane, and because the events of the physical plane can be manipulated to reflect astral reality, sooner or later, you will find yourself with more money.

Try several exercises using visualizations. Remember, you define your own reality. The visualization exercises are intended to introduce you to the theory and practice of visualization, and as such, they are basic exercises. Once you learn how to visualize you can use what you learn to start changing your world. Your imagination is not something that holds you back, and it is not a waste of time to exercise it. Imagination is one of the *tools* you will learn to use to create change and to make things happen in your life. The point is, whatever goes on in your imagination is actually happening to you. It is part of your reality.

Right now, imagine that you are walking alone down a darkened street in a dangerous part of town. You hear footsteps behind you, and it sounds as though the person following you is walking faster and getting closer. As you imagine, your heart begins to race, your pulse speeds up, and your blood pressure rises perceptibly. You are frightened, even though you sit in the safety of your own living room! Your own physical reality has just been created by your imagination.

Everything in the universe consists of energy. Visualization allows you to tap into this energy and allows you to manipulate energy as well. You can attract those things you would like to have in your life, and repel those things you no longer want as part of your reality.

Another thing you need to be aware of is *how* you visualize. You are using your psychic sight (**clairvoyance**) when you visualize, and that process does not involve your eyes as physical sight does. If you expect visualization to be something like watching a movie on a little screen somewhere in front of your face, you will find it difficult to visualize. Everyone processes psychic sight in a different way. Release those expectations, and allow your psychic vision to manifest in whatever way is appropriate for you. As you try the various exercises, you will be able to easily and effortlessly find the best way for you to visualize - unless you insist on it happening in a certain way!

Some processes that require effort in the physical world are easily accomplished, or not required at all, when you visualize. For example, climbing a mountain in the physical world can be exhausting to those in good physical condition or might be impossible for those who are disabled. In a visualization, everyone moves from place to place easily and without exertion. If you are visualizing a meadow, for example, and you want to cross it, you simply will yourself to be on the other side. There is no need to plod across the terrain a step at a time as if you are in the physical world. To move in a visualization, *be* in the new location using thought. Your mind has enormous power: use it!

Remember that if you insist on telling yourself that you cannot visualize, you are absolutely right. You can do only what you believe you can do.

You will find it difficult if not impossible to visualize effectively if you are not relaxed, centered, and grounded.

Visualizations are best done when you can choose a place and time when you will be alone and undisturbed. Close the door, turn off the television and radio, and unplug the phone. If you cannot be alone and undisturbed at home, drive into the country and find a quiet place in the woods or a meadow, or simply park your car in the shade somewhere away from traffic, roll up the windows, and use your car as your own quiet place! Automobile seats today are quite comfortable, and the car itself is soundproofed. Sit on the passenger side to enjoy the extra space. Of course, always choose a place that is safe. If you are at all uncomfortable about sitting alone on the edge of a country road, you will not be able to visualize effectively.

Creative Visualization Exercise - The Meadow

This is a basic visualization that I use in my classes. While reading through it, you might notice that you are instructed to walk across the meadow. References to moving through space in a physical sense are included in case you find it difficult to visualize yourself moving instantly from here to there. The best way is to "pop" from place to place instantly, the way Samantha does it in the TV series "Bewitched." If you can visualize yourself moving in that way, then disregard the instructions to walk anywhere and just zap yourself from place to place! Remember, in your imagination, you can do anything that Samantha does!

🕮 Sit comfortably in a position that supports your head and body or lie down. Close your eyes and relax your eyelids.

🕮 Begin breathing slowly, deeply, rhythmically, and deliberately.

🕮 Tighten and then relax all of the muscles in your body. You can do them all at once, or you can start at one end of the body and progress to the other end. Visualize your tension as dark, heavy energy and let it drain down into the chair or bed and then into the earth. Imagine it being pulled down into the center of the earth and being cleansed and diffused as clear white energy through the earth's crust.

🕮 Deepen your state of concentration and relaxation by entering an elevator and watching the numbers change floor by floor, from the 21st floor where you boarded, until you reach the first floor. The doors open and you see a beautiful country meadow. The lush green grass is dotted with dozens of multicolored flowers; there are mountains in the distance and the sky overhead is a vivid blue. You can hear bees as they go about their work and see butterflies dart from flower to flower. Continue listening and you hear birds singing. Hear one bird call to another and hear the second bird answer. The sun is warm and a sweet-smelling breeze is gently blowing.

Now be there, standing in the meadow. You are barefoot. Feel the grass, warm and soft beneath your feet. Begin walking through the meadow, noticing the various flowers and enjoying the sensation of the warm sun on your head, shoulders, and back. Start walking easily and comfortably towards the forest in the distance.

Now you are approaching a tumbling brook that runs through the meadow. As you get near, you can hear the water cascading over the rocks in the stream bed. The water is clear and you can see the sand and rocks in the bottom of the stream. Sit on a smooth rock at the edge of the stream and dip your bare feet into the cool, refreshing water. Feel the water rippling around your feet and ankles, tickling your toes and caressing your skin. Reach down and wet your fingertips; taste the cool water. Inhale and smell the cool refreshing air around you.

Arise now. You feel very relaxed and deeply contented. In the distance, you see a forest. Walk now towards the forest, moving along at a comfortable pace. The pines and hemlocks are blowing gently in the breeze, and you can smell their soft scent. Sunlight filters down through the trees. You feel a sense of anticipation. A being waits for you at the forest's edge. As you draw closer, you can determine facial features. This is one of your guides. Feel the love emanating from this being who has been waiting for you; feel the safety and protection that is offered. Greet your guide now, as you are greeted in return. You can ask a question if you wish, or you can simply enjoy the feeling of companionship and love that surrounds you - there are no expectations. You both sit in the warm soft grass under a tree, and your guide places a warm hand over yours. If this is your first meeting, just sit back and enjoy the silent companionship; if you have been here before, you can ask questions of your guide, request guidance, or simply converse as friends.

When you feel that your meeting with your guide has been satisfactory, rise to your feet, bid your guide goodbye, being sure to offer thanks for the help that was given to you, and, with the feeling of great love surrounding you, begin to walk back out into the meadow. In the distance ahead you can see the doors to the elevator and you easily cross the short distance to them. Board the elevator again, watch the doors close on your meadow, and now watch the numbers light up as the elevator rises up from the first floor back up to floor 21. When the doors open on the 21st floor, you will retain the feeling of rejuvenation and love that you felt in the meadow. You are still completely relaxed, yet you feel vigorously energized.

Open your eyes slowly and sit quietly for a few moments before going back to your daily life.

Remember that your peaceful meadow and the wisdom of your guide are only a few moments away and are always available to you.

a list of conditions that have to be satisfied, the thoughtform cannot work in an optimum way.

When it has accomplished the results you want, the thoughtform ceases to exist. If you want to work further, you will have to create another thoughtform.

If you change your mind after creating a thoughtform and no longer want to use it, just visualize your thoughtform falling from space into the ocean. The energy you created is used to help the earth in some way.

If Your Thoughtform Does Not Work

Thoughtforms do not work if:

☆ Your intention in creating it is not clear

☆ You try to work with more than one thoughtform at a time

☆ Your intent is manipulative

☆ You do not allow enough time for it to work

☆ You impose conditions that made it impossible to achieve what you want

☆ You worry about the results, or about whether it can work at all

Try again. Build another thoughtform, this time putting as much energy into its creation as you can. Be very clear about what it is that you want to happen. Take more time with the visualization; this is the easiest part of the whole process. Do not worry about results or how they will occur; allow the thoughtform to do its work in the best way possible. You can visualize the thoughtform in a humanized way, if that helps. I have used elves, gnomes, and other elementals as starting points for thoughtforms. Use what works!

9

Karma

Each thought, action, or word is composed of energy, and energy is governed by universal principles. Energy is defined by *movement*. If a thing does not move, it has no energy, and in a broad sense, does not exist. Therefore, thoughts, actions, and words (and everything else we are aware of) have movement. When you have a thought, the energy of that thought moves outward from your aura and is registered somewhere. This registry is often called the **akashic record**.

The **akashic realm** is a vibration higher than the spiritual and angelic realms. Its purpose is to store information in the form of energy. The term **akasha** is defined as life force or the state of being alive. If you pick up a fossil of a dinosaur bone and receive information about the animal that it once was part of when it was alive, you are reading the akasha (life force) that still exists in the fossil. Every movement, action, or thought that the animal had during its life is recorded in the akashic record and is connected to, and therefore available through, the fossil. The fossil can be used as a *tool* to access the information stored in the akashic records. The pages of this book contain the akashic record of the trees from which they were made.

Every thought, every action, every word that you have had, done, or said in your lifetime is captured in the same way that a voice is recorded on an audio tape, stored in the akashic records, and thus can be played back or recalled. Sobering thought, isn't it? Even more sobering is the thought that if any one person can access this source of information, then so can anyone else. (There are some restrictions, however, that prevent others from obtaining information that your higher self has determined to be yours alone.)

The physical movement of the vocal chords is deciphered by the moving recording head mechanism of the tape recorder, which then stores the energy it picked up on a moving section of tape. If you hold an audio tape in your hand, you hear nothing... but the voice has been recorded on that tape anyway. If you put the tape on an audio tape player, you can once again hear the voice that was recorded. The akashic records work in the same way. The information has been recorded. You just need to learn how to play it back. That is what psychic development is all about.

Using logic, you can assume that it would be pointless to record all of this information somewhere if it was not going to be used for some purpose. Our higher selves use the akashic records in a number of ways. One of the most important ways is to register information to be used for learning and growth. **Memory** is nothing more than the process of accessing information stored in the akashic records.

Karma is the process by which the higher self learns and grows. It plays back the information that was recorded in the akashic record and sets up scenarios for that part of itself which is a physically incarnated person (you) that will help it experience something more about a given topic.

Eastern religions have been much more aware of how karma works than have those in the west. Unfortunately, however, the aspect of karma that seems to get most distorted in the transition from eastern concept to western comprehension of the concept is that karma is a *payback or punishment* system. Part of the problem is that a person trained in western thought cannot fully understand eastern theologies. The cultures are simply too different, and westerners have been trained to look at life from a specific viewpoint. This viewpoint is different from that held by those raised in the eastern countries. And, as with any theological school of thought, distortion naturally occurs over time, separating truth and knowledge from the concept.

Karma is not a matter of payback like the Old Testament "eye for an eye" system of thought, because there is no scale on which to measure the true worth of anything in a meaningful way. Nor is it a matter of punishment, the concept that a wrongdoer will be wronged as a result of his initial action, simply because he did wrong. Both of these concepts are gross oversimplifications of a complex universal truth.

Karma is more a *cause and effect* system. Every thought, action, or word that you release into the cosmos and that is recorded in the akashic record has an impact somewhere, even if you are unaware of it. Drop a pebble in a pond and, sooner or later, a wave caused by the pebble will wash onto the beach. In the same way, the "waves" sent out by your thought, action, or word cause something to happen somewhere else in the cosmos. There is an effect registered somewhere; the "disturbance" out there somewhere beyond your consciousness causes something else to happen. If you drop a pebble in a small, quiet pond, and wait long enough, you will eventually see the wave sent out by the pebble rebound off the shore and make its way back to its origin. At the same time, it reverberates in other directions, setting up quite a disturbance on the water's surface.

If you want to see this concept illustrated, find a small shallow container of water, about as big as a birdbath. Drop a small pebble directly into the center, and watch the one small wave it creates become an enormous network of waves as it issues forth from the site where the pebble was dropped and then bounces back from the outside edge of the container. In a matter of seconds, the entire surface of the water is agitated.

You are the pebble. You are also the beach.

That is karma.

It is important to understand the concept of karma in this real way, a way that can be easily demonstrated and grasped by a mind trained in western consciousness. It illustrates the idea that every thought, every action, every word has an impact *somewhere*, even if you do not see it from your limited perspective.

Just as the wave that the pebble produced is exactly the same wave that returns to the site where the pebble is dropped, the energy that you originally send out by your action, thought, or words is exactly the same as that which comes rebounding back to you. If it is positive energy, what comes back to you is positive. If it is manipulative or negative, that is what you get back in your own life.

Many metaphysical systems allow for this amplification effect. Because your single small action reverberates energetically in *all* directions, the energy increases over time. So, you will find that if you send out some positive energy, you will see several positive effects returned as a result.

One interesting metaphysical concept takes into account the incredible wisdom and perception of your higher self. Because it knows that the same negativity that you send out returns to you, your higher self very often filters that energy for you.

In other words, if you deliberately try to be manipulative, your higher self, in an attempt to protect you to some degree, ensures that the energy you send out is short-circuited. Those who try to manipulate circumstances or issues for their own gain find themselves unable to make it work, and those who are manipulative find that their victims frequently disappear from their lives.

10

Reincarnation and Past Life Regression

You are much, much more than a physical being. That which defines "you" consists primarily of energy. Just as no two physical beings are exactly alike (including identical twins, who have different fingerprints, voice pitches, and so on), no two souls are alike. Each person's energy exists at a specific frequency that defines that person.

The purpose of life in the physical plane is to gather experience. In order to gain experience in those areas upon which you want to focus, your higher self gathers together specific qualities and projects them into physical form in a process called **incarnation**. The portion sent down (or **invested**) in the physical body forms your personality and ego consciousness. The portion that remains in nonphysical form is called the **higher self**, or **over-soul**.

While it is sharing the physical body, the invested part of the soul usually occupies the area of the crown chakra at the top of the head, which is why we associate our consciousness with our head or brain. When the body alters its state of perception, such as when you are deeply asleep, meditating, or comatose, the soul is freed from the physical and reconnects with the higher self portion. During these times, learning takes place as the energy of the invested soul interacts with the energy of the higher self. Those people who feel disconnected from life are the ones whose soul is not assimilating the higher self energy in an optimum way.

In each lifetime, a different set of qualities is focused in your consciousness. In the same way that you do not look the same in various incarnations because you do not have the same physical body, you also are not the same person either, because your invested soul is composed of different aspects of your total being. In that sense, those beings who came before were completely different people. In essence, however, your soul is the creator of all of those people, and it is through this connection that we are able to regress into past lives to gain some perception of what our higher self has been learning and focusing on in its various incarnations.

Reincarnation is the repetition of this process. Each time you incarnate, you do so for different purposes. Your higher self might choose to work on some of the same topics in different lifetimes, but because the people around you are different each time, these topics are experienced in a different way. Through this process you will be able to experience all possible facets of some aspect of life and learning. This is true freedom. In each lifetime you can do exactly as you choose, because in others, you can make other choices!

When you die, the part of your soul essence that you have invested in a physical body is released and is able to return to the higher self. If you have lived your life with awareness, you will have been in contact in some way with your higher self. Living in a spiritual way raises your vibration, and one of the benefits of being aware of your higher self occurs when you die. The higher your vibration has been raised during your life, the faster you will ascend to your higher self, and the more energy you will be able to take with you. We use the term "ascend" because after physical death, your soul has to journey through the various planes of existence until it reaches the higher vibration of the spiritual planes, and in doing so, its vibration has to increase in order to pass "upwards" to the next plane of existence. In each plane, the soul is cleansed and energized. The negativity that you embraced during your physical life has to be left behind on these lower planes because it cannot exist in the rarefied vibration of the higher planes. Only your positive aspects can accompany you back to the spiritual planes. Therefore, those leading a very negative life will have to spend more time in each of the lower planes as this cleansing takes place.

That which is called Hell (or Purgatory, or the Winterlands, or something else depending on the particular religious tradition you follow) exists in the middle astral plane. It is in this realm where negativity is experienced most strongly, because it can exist only in the etheric or lower astral realms to any degree. Negativity is cleansed and released by reviewing the experience and understanding all aspects of it. Someone who was full of hate and fear in physical life will find an astral world filled with things to hate and fear. Those who victimize during their physical life will find an abundance of beings who return that lesson in negativity. Some souls even become stuck in the etheric or lower astral worlds because their death was sudden, violent, or occurred while they were in a highly emotional state. They are simply unaware that death has occurred, and continue as if they remained alive. This causes confusion when they no longer have an effect upon their world, and it is this confusion that lengthens their stay in these realms. It is much the same as the phenomenon people report when they lose a limb. They can continue to "feel" the limb long after it is physically gone. The astral representation of that limb still exists because imperfection does not exist in the astral realm. Kirlian photographs of a leaf which has been cut in half show that the energy of the *entire* leaf remains even though physically, half of the leaf is gone. The Kirlian photograph shows the outline of the entire leaf.

Although only past lives are discussed in this chapter, understand that theoretically, there is nothing to prevent you from examining *future lives* as well. In the time/space continuum in which we exist, it is believed in many metaphysical circles that "all time is now." If one accepts that theory, there is nothing to prevent movement and exploration in either direction!

Soul Groups

Throughout your many incarnations, you have probably been associated with the same large group of beings known as a **soul group**. There are many soul groups, and although we can freely move between the various groups, we generally remain with the same group of souls, loving and learning together. Among the members of a soul group there is a mutual contract to help other members with some aspect of learning. We get the same consideration in return. So, each and every person in your life, without exception, is a member of your soul group, and is there for two purposes: to help you with some aspect of your life and to receive help from you on some aspect of their own life. Many kinds of lessons are learned in tandem with others. This includes both the people you love and those you dislike.

One easy way that I use to deal with people I am not very fond of is to affirm that they are part of my soul group, and that they are in my life so that I can learn something from them. When we consider that these people are valuable allies on our soul's journey, it makes it easier to tolerate them in our day-to-day lives. **Affirmations** work very well in this case as long as you actually believe what you are affirming. They have no value at all if you are just saying them without any conviction.

The concept of soul groups can explain those occasions when, upon meeting someone for the first time, you feel that you have met before and have forgotten their name or when you are surprised at the depth of the attraction that exists between you and this new person. If you have worked with the essence of this person before, in another physical existence, you (or more accurately, the invested part of your soul) can recognize that essence, even though the physical body and personality are different. This information comes directly from your higher self. That you can sense the connection gives you an idea of how strong the energy must be, and of how much the higher self wants you to understand that this is indeed a person with whom you will work in this lifetime.

Spiritual Guides

While we, as a soul group, continue to incarnate into the physical plane, other beings regularly incarnate into higher realms. While our incarnational purpose is to learn in the physical world - the realm of limitations - theirs is to provide guidance to those of us who choose to learn on lower vibrational planes by helping maintain our life plan throughout our incarnation. Your higher self designed this life plan before your physical birth, and after your physical death you review both the plan and your physical life to see how you have progressed.

These guides work with you each night when you are in a deep sleep. If you deliberately develop a sensitivity to their presence, they can also contact you during more conscious times, such as when you meditate. By accessing their guidance you can accelerate your growth. They have the advantage of being able to easily confer with their own higher selves because they exist in an energy vibration (a **realm**) which is much higher than the frequency of the earth plane, and therefore much closer to the vibration of the spiritual realms. The guides in turn receive guidance from the plane immediately above theirs, the **angelic realm**.

Your guides do not direct your life. Their purpose is to help you maintain your focus on your incarnational plan, should you desire their help. Those people who do not actively and consciously seek the help of their guides are most likely doing so while they sleep and, therefore, do not recall the experience. The value in consciously seeking guidance is that the guide's wisdom and aid can be more directly accessed. Consciousness implies focus; any topic upon which you focus during your lifetime is important for soul growth.

If you consider a guide to be nothing more than a very dear and close friend, you can more likely access the guide's energy. Remember, a guide does not direct your life. They do not tell us what to do, what choice to make, or how to live. Guides have a higher level of perception about your life, since they exist in a higher vibration, and they realize that you are incarnated only to learn. How you learn a lesson is your own decision.

If you create a crisis in your life and then expect your guides to magically intercede and get you out of the situation, you will find that this is not their purpose. Instead, perhaps your own higher self will "guide" you out of the situation, frequently putting you into a more uncomfortable one in order to urge you to deal with it. Or perhaps you will get no guidance whatsoever. Sometimes an issue can be temporarily resolved simply by floundering about for a while until we suddenly find ourselves in another situation which demands more attention. It is like a freshly caught fish wriggling around on the shore. The fish can either end up back in the water or further away from the pond. A great amount of energy is used up in the process. Accessing the wisdom and love of guides helps us to conserve this otherwise wasted energy!

Past Lives

You are, at this moment, the sum total of all of the experiences of all of your past lives. That total also includes the experience gained while in spiritual realms during those periods between physical lifetimes. Your present incarnational plan was devised based on the experiences of all of these past lives. By understanding them, we can understand our incarnational plan in this lifetime. We are also able to see where growth has occurred.

Recalling past lives has proven extremely helpful in uncovering the origins of phobias, compulsions, and illnesses. Our lives mirror our experience. If you are afraid of heights, for example, the reason might be that you fell to your death from a cliff in another life. A fear of water can be traced back to a drowning in another life. Once we understand the source of a problem, it becomes much easier to release that negative energy from our life. It is unreasonable to believe that what occurred in one lifetime will occur again in another - unless you are going through life so unfocused and unaware that you must repeat certain experiences just so you notice that something is happening to you!

We can also use past life recall to trace the positive aspects of our present lives. A love of the ocean, for example, might be traced back to a highly rewarding and enjoyable life spent on or near the sea. We can trace other lifetimes with a loved one to find out how and why such a strong bond was formed. As a general rule, the people who are strongly in your life - the people with whom you connect emotionally - have been with you before in other lives. That includes family, lovers, close friends, and occasionally co-workers. Those people we consider acquaintances, or with whom we have no emotional bond, are either coming into our soul group for the first time, or are here in some way to teach us about some minor aspect of life and will then move on to someone else. This is a mutual process, so in the same way that others are in our lives to help us, so are we there to help others. Chance meetings always have significance. If you treat each person you meet as if they are in your life to impart some special gift, you will develop sufficient awareness to easily be able to see exactly why they are there.

There is an easy technique that can illustrate to us how we looked physically in another life. It is an interesting experiment, but it has limited usefulness. Although it is enjoyable to see what we looked like in other lifetimes, the technique by itself does not bring us an appreciation for who that person was in his or her life. In order to reexperience ourselves in other lifetimes, it is necessary to perform a full past life regression.

Past Life Regression Exercise

Place a candle between your face and a mirror in a darkened room. The candle should be throwing light on your face from either side, but the flame should not be in your direct line of vision. Do not place the candle below your chin or above your forehead because the light that it casts will artificially change your features.

Open your crown chakra and circulate energy down into your heart chakra. Fix your eyes on your face in the mirror. Unfocus your eyes as you did to see auras. Do not blink at this point. Hold the gaze, and in a few moments, while your vibration is being raised through the energy entering the crown chakra, your face will begin to darken and fade as you watch. In a moment or two, it will be replaced *briefly* by another face: you, in another lifetime!

The impression, as with most psychic impressions, will be fleeting. Blinking your eyes is a physical reaction used to refocus the eyes, so it will prevent the image from fully forming. Once it forms, however, you can close your eyes to retain the image without losing it. Again, attitude plays an important role in determining how successful this experiment will be. As with other psychic endeavors, do not stop the flow of energy by *willing* it to happen. Simply sit expectantly and *know* that it will occur!

You might have to try this exercise several times before you achieve success.

What if you see something ugly or negative? That occasionally happens, and it is important to understand why. No, it is not spooks or negative entities playing tricks on you! A natural energy barrier blankets the physical plane. This prevents us from moving our energy too far from the physical world. We are here because right now, we belong here, by our own choice. This energy barrier serves to protect both serious students of higher awareness and the less evolved curiosity seekers from exceeding their own limitations.

If you see something negative - whatever that means to you - pay attention to the warning you receive. It is simply a message from your higher self that you are moving into an area that you are either not ready to deal with or not equipped to handle. As with everything in life, you can only do what you are ready and able to do, and this preparation comes from past lives and also from abilities gained in this lifetime. For example, you cannot design a spaceship just because you want to. In the same way, you cannot access higher realms just because you want to. You have to raise your energy, your vibration, through practice and experience. Negative images, therefore, are nothing more than warnings to tread slowly because you are in an area where you are not yet equipped to deal with what you may uncover. Pay attention and slow down!

And, as with anything metaphysical, if the techniques you use create chaos or an uncomfortable feeling, do something else. Metaphysics incorporates a number of tools used for growth and learning. These are joyous processes! If something is not working, perhaps the timing of having that life experience is not best for you, or perhaps you would learn something that is inappropriate, or maybe you are just not able to work well with that particular energy. If you do not sense joy and love in the process, it simply means your higher self is not cooperating. Your higher self sets the direction for your life. Its wisdom and direction can be observed in those areas of your life where you feel loved and happy. Although you can learn from a negative process, it is far easier to learn from positive experiences!

Techniques for Past Life Regression

Sit comfortably with head and body completely supported, or lie on a bed or on a mat on the floor. Since you will be relatively immobile for a period of about half an hour, be sure to wear loose, comfortable, warm clothing. Remember to lock the doors, disconnect the phone, turn off the television - in fact, do everything you can to ensure that you will be undisturbed for a period of about one hour. If you live in a chaotic household where you know you will not be able to be undisturbed for that long a period of time, then take a drive in your car to an area where you can pull the car safely and completely off the road. A pleasant country road or a scenic lookout are good choices. Make sure the area you choose is a safe one. Sit on the passenger side if it is more comfortable. Adjust the temperature, recline the seats if possible; do whatever you can to make the experience more enjoyable. You will obtain better results.

Understand, before you begin, that the state that you will enter in order to view past lives is a light hypnotic trance. Almost everyone is capable of being hypnotized. It is true that some people can achieve deeper trance states than others; it is also true that some people can enter the trance state more easily than others. Aside from the possible benefits of performing past life regressions, the ability to easily hypnotize oneself comes in handy in many other situations, such as a visit to the dentist. It is a great way to reduce pain and stress levels and to reduce the fear reaction that many of us experience as we hear the dentist's drill!

There are three methods commonly used to perform a past life regression. The most evidential is **self-regression**. In early attempts, you will need help to achieve a trance state deep enough so that you will be able to return information. As you progress, however, you will find that you can achieve a deeper state of relaxation and still retain enough control to handle the regression alone.

The second method is an **assisted self-regression**. This is the easiest way for a beginner to experience past life regression. This can be somewhat less evidential because the directions are being given by someone who cannot also view your past life at the same time. It is very difficult to ask the correct questions and occasionally information may be missed or ignored or considered insignificant by the regressor. However, it is far easier than attempting to work alone in your first few attempts, and it actually allows you to reexperience the life that you are describing. You need to work with someone you trust in order to gain maximum benefit from the regression.

The third method is a **past life reading** performed by a third party who is psychic and who has experience in performing past life regressions. That person will describe your past lives to you. This is probably the least evidential because you are not truly involved in the regression, and you just have to accept the reader's word for what they see or experience. It also cheats you of the thrill of returning to another existence, it does very little to improve your psychic skills, and it can be expensive. I recommend this method only when other attempts to do a self-regression, whether alone or assisted, have failed.

However, it is easy enough to regress yourself. By viewing past lives again, we can learn a great deal of information about ourselves and our current lives.

Following are two past life regression methods. Both are similar in technique, but the information you receive will be obtained in different ways.

Using the first method, you regress yourself into a past life and by answering questions, you can vocalize the experiences of that life. If this experience is recorded, you can study it later with the intent of using the tape as a trigger for further remembrance. You can use this method any number of times and return to as many other life experiences as you choose.

The other method allows you to scan several lives for significant experiences. You will have a definite feeling which method seems the best way, so ask yourself which method will work best for you, clear your mind, relax, and wait for the answer.

You can perform either method using the help of your spirit guide. Simply visualize your guide walking towards you before you view a past life experience. Your guide is there to help you learn more about your past life experiences; if you want this help, you have only to ask for it. In this case, allow your guide to do what they do best - *guide* you back to those past lives in which you learned or experienced that which will help you most in this life. Remember, the guide was present during these other lives!

You can also view those lives in which you experienced that which affects you the most deeply in your present life. If you want to explore the relationship you have with someone you love in this life, you can trace your relationship back through other lives. You can find the source of compulsions and phobias. The information you need is always available to you; can obtain it simply by wanting to remember it.

It is a good practice to carefully consider what areas of your life you want to study in regard to past life influence and then direct the regression in a way that addresses the issues about which you want more information. Attempting to see all of your past lives, or to view a group of unconnected lives, will most likely result in very little real evidence. Starting a regression with "I want to see some of my past lives" will produce very little valuable or usable information. A better method is to focus on some topic that you want clarification; for example: "show me one of my past lives that will help explain why I am afraid of high places." By focusing your search in this way, you can eliminate receiving images of other lives that have no bearing on the topics that interest you.

If you want to work alone, you can tape the regressions and play them back for further study. A second tape recorder is required if you want to tape your responses to the questions you record on the regression tape. You also have to remember, when recording the material which you will play back for yourself when you actually regress, to leave long pauses when you ask a question. Information does not come through quickly, and you need to anticipate that it may take you a minute or two to get the answer to the question being posed, and another minute or two to describe your answer. If you do not leave significant time lapses between questions, you will feel rushed when you regress, and the resulting frustration will definitely affect the validity and value of the information you receive. So, take your time! Understand that you will be attempting to relive an entire lifetime in the space of thirty or forty minutes, and you need to allow your subconscious sufficient time to process out the insignificant and the inconsequential as it searches for the important and illuminating moments of that life.

You can ask a friend who has a calm and soothing yet energetic voice to either record the questions, or to sit with you and ask the questions directly. This person should be someone who is supportive of the work, and someone with whom you can feel free to say anything. Very often, the information in past life regressions is of a negative nature - some aspect of life was badly handled in that one, and that negative experience is now being processed and something of value is being found in it. If you are reticent about voicing negative qualities about yourself, you will tend to hold back information that might be valuable. If this is the case, do yourself a favor and work with a tape recorded regression.

Obviously, regressions should be approached with a positive attitude. You have lived before, but you have not always been an enlightened person in all of those lives. Have the courage to face the fact that you might view aspects of yourself that are less than desirable or which you want to deny in your current life. There is a chance that in some past life you were a thief, a murderer, a prostitute - all of those aspects of life which are with us always. The point is, if you lived those aspects before, you do not have to live them again! You experienced that part of yourself and now you can concentrate on other things.

It is best not to become too involved in this lifetime with reprocessing who or what you were in other lives. Let the information come to you so that you can learn and benefit from it, and then just let it go. After all, the person you will see was a part of your self, with all of your many strengths and faults. Your strength in this life frequently comes from accepting yourself in all of your aspects. Dealing with your faults allows those experiences to become strengths. The experience will be beneficial to you regardless of what you see, but regressing with a positive outlook enables you to recall more of the positive from other lives, and this will help you to see your strengths and positive aspects in this life!

Remember also that you will be completely safe during the entire regression. No harm can come to you. Events of that life will be replayed for you for your good and so that you may learn from them. Your emotions are not connected to the personality that was you in the other lifetime. You are safe where you are, in your current life; you cannot be harmed or frightened by anything that happens to you in that lifetime.

For this reason, do not be afraid to experience your death in that lifetime again as you regress. You will not actually die again in this lifetime, and the death experience from any lifetime can hold immense power because it seems to be the point at which you view the most complete and understanding picture of that lifetime.

Also be aware that you can never enter a trance or hypnotic state that is too deep. The deeper your trance, the easier it becomes to dissociate with your present life and to bring back clearer details from other lives. You cannot become stuck in a trance state, unable to awaken. In any case, the absolute worst that will happen is that you will simply fall asleep and awaken shortly thereafter feeling refreshed and invigorated. Should this happen, just remember when you regress again that you allowed yourself to relax too much, and your subconscious will automatically adjust the level of your trance.

Regressing to a Significant Past Life Exercise

☼ Relax, center, and ground yourself. Breathe in slowly, hold your breath, and then breathe out.

☼ Picture yourself in an outdoor place that is very special to you. If it exists in reality, go there in your mind. You can see it again. If you cannot easily picture such a place, then imagine one. It is a very beautiful and relaxing place. The sun shines overhead, a gentle breeze blows, and you can hear birds call to their mates in the distance. Hear, feel, smell - BE in this place now.

☼ A flash of blinding light draws your attention. Directly ahead of you, a large golden door has appeared. As you walk towards it, the door begins to open slowly, and by the time you stand before it, the door is completely open.

Reincarnation and Past Life Regression / 93

You can see a swirling violet mist behind the door, and as you pass through the portal, the mist envelops you in welcoming warmth.

🔔 Another flash of light. You are standing in a place where you have lived before. You are viewing this life from the perspective of someone who has lived it fully.

🔔 Look at your clothing. Look down at your feet and describe what you are wearing on them.

☆ What country are you living in?

☆ Who is the ruler of this country?

☆ What is the date? The month and year?

☆ Which gender are you?

☆ What kind of work do you do?

☆ How old are you?

☆ Do you have brothers or sisters? How many? What are their names?

☆ Describe your appearance.

☆ Did you ever marry? What was your spouse's name? What was that person like? Can you describe that person?

☆ Did you have children? What were their names and genders?

☆ Was your life generally happy or unhappy?

☆ How did you die?

☆ What was the most important lesson that you gained from that lifetime?

☆ Was anyone in your present life experience with you in that lifetime? What was your relationship then?

☆ What lesson or work are you attempting to complete in your present life?

📖 Allow yourself a few moments to fully appreciate the person you were in this past existence. Are there any traits that you notice in yourself today?

📖 As the violet mist begins to rise around you once again, you know that you are about to leave this place. Leave behind you some positive energy and love; visualize the place filling with white light.

Scanning A Past Life for Details

Instead of doing a complete past life regression - in which you can gather an enormous amount of information - you can also limit the experience to gain information only about a specific topic. For example, if you are trying to understand why you are overweight, learning about your interaction with brothers and sisters and knowing who ruled the country in a past life can be considered unnecessary. Those details do not help you understand the topic about which you are primarily interested. Limiting a regression to only that information that can help answer your question is called **scanning**.

Perform the regression in the same way, but before you begin, focus on the topic that interests you and direct yourself to receive only information that will be helpful to understand that topic.

Considerations for Past Life Regressions

Cover one topic at a time. If you have several areas of interest, perform a past life regression for each topic.

As with any work in the psychic fields, you might have to do several regressions before you begin to receive valid information. Keep trying!

If you do not tape record the experience, write down your impressions as soon as you finish the regression. Information gathered in the alpha state is fleeting; your memory of the experience will be reduced by each minute that passes.

If you choose to work with someone else, be sure that the other person is someone you trust and with whom you can share your experiences. Nothing is more frustrating than gathering a great deal of helpful information about a past life and then not being able to share it with your companion because you are not comfortable discussing the kind of person you were in that particular life. *All* of us have had lives in which we were murderers, prostitutes, or thieves. Your values and morals in this life are a reflection of what you learned by experience in other lives. If you cannot deal with the concept that you were not always the same as you are today, then it can be difficult to share many of your past lives with others.

Is it a genuine past life that you are recalling or just your imagination? Do not dismiss your experiences to imagination. If it feels like a genuine memory, then it probably is.

If you find a number of lives in which you were prosperous or famous, stop regressing and start thinking instead about why you seem to receive only information about those types of lives. Your ego is directing these regressions. Try to figure out why you have such a deep need to be rich or famous or loved by millions. Most of our lives are ordinary. Look around you: how many people do you know who are rich or famous? If you consider every person you have met, you probably have a pool of hundreds to consider. Half a dozen of them might have exceptional lives. Apply the same ratio to your own past lives. The numbers will match up. There is much more useful information to be discovered in the past lives of ordinary people.

11

Healing

Healing is part of what the New Age is all about. At this stage of our development, we can look around and see the ravages of our past as they exist in our present. And we can repair much of the damage by using psychic healing techniques.

Although some people experience an improvement in the condition of their physical bodies after a psychic healing, it is **not** the physical with which we are concerned. Psychic healing works on the energy bodies.

For legal reasons (specifically medical malpractice, which applies to everyone - not just physicians - and the laws apply whether you were paid or did the work without charging for it), **never** give anyone the idea, either by direct statement or implication, that your psychic healing work will improve any physical condition from which they suffer. Although they may experience a change in their physical condition, it is illegal almost everywhere in the United States of America to make such a claim. Be aware that the penalties for doing so are severe. Making these claims is also completely unethical. Remember, ethics and karma work in tandem. Your ethical (and unethical) behavior creates karma. Make sure it is the kind of karma you want to work with, either in this or in a future lifetime!

Psychic healing is intended to be used for **self-healing**. You cannot heal others until your own life is in good condition. What happens instead is that you can exchange some of your imperfect energy and the other person might begin to see the effects of that in his or her life. That is not what healing is all about.

Dis-ease occurs when the energy bodies, including the physical, are stressed in inappropriate ways. Illness occurs first in the etheric body and even before it is discernible there, we can see impending illness in the colors of the astral body. We draw illness into the physical body by blocking the flow of energy. We can heal our energy bodies by transforming energy. We replace undesirable or negative energy patterns with positive, beneficial frequencies.

There are many techniques for healing. If you are interested in this field you can seek out further information from books or from people who have experience in healing. Each healer has his or her own technique that might or might not work for someone else. Try a number of techniques with which you feel comfortable and use those with which you have the best results.

Various techniques include the use of crystals, music, color, and so forth. These are **tools** that you use to accomplish your goal. They have no value in and of themselves. A crystal, by itself, is a rock. A crystal used by someone who knows how to direct and control energy effectively is a tool that allows the healer to focus his attention and his energy. It remains, as it always will, a rock. It is *you* who is manipulating your energy and causing something to happen. Your primary interest does not lie in the crystal - it lies in the transmutation of energy that you accomplish using the crystal as your tool.

Remember that in performing psychic healing on a physical body, do **not** diagnose illness. If someone is ill, their first responsibility to themselves is to seek medical help. Legally, you cannot make any effort to diagnose without running the risk of being sued for medical malpractice. Even if your diagnosis happens to be correct, it is still illegal. And in this case, good intentions definitely do not count!

Psychic healing is done in an effort to help the person's body learn to more effectively transfer energy and to remove energy blockages. Let those who have knowledge in medical treatment do their part. Your part is much different and is valuable in an entirely different way. It is important to remember that by the time illness has manifested in the physical body, it is the result of a serious energy problem. To rid the person of the problem, we need to treat the process in reverse. Getting rid of the densest energy blockages first by medically treating the physical body provides immediate help. That is the primary concern for anyone who is ill enough to seek help. When the condition of their physical body has improved, then it is appropriate to be concerned with their energetic bodies in order to remove the root cause of the illness and to prevent its recurrence. You should take care to remind the person you are healing of those facts. My advice is to *never* perform a psychic healing on anyone who refuses to seek and follow through with medical help *first*. A healing will not work for anyone who allows a medical condition to persist. If they will not use their own energy to take care of themselves, they will not accept the same energy from you, and no healing will result.

Also, do not offer psychic healing to anyone by stating that using such a technique would be to their benefit. It is ethical to mention that you would like to help them using psychic healing techniques, but make sure that your offer is stated as being something that *you* want to do, and that you make no claims about any benefits that may occur as a result of your action. Your higher self will bring to you those who need your help, and they will ask for it on their own. Those who seem disinterested must be allowed to follow their own path. Be sure to review the chapter on ethics before you do any psychic healing work.

Methods for Psychic Healing

Chakra Balancing - Visualize the chakras moving into alignment; when the person seems to be centered and grounded, visualize colors flowing into each chakra. Most healers use the rainbow color assignments, starting with red at the base chakra and ending with purple at the crown chakra. Use whatever color system seems appropriate. Different colors might apply to different people. Visualize the energy of each chakra turning in a clockwise motion. Chakra energies look like small whirlwinds or tornadoes.

Color Therapy - Intuitively sense the absence or abundance of color in each chakra. Visualize color being added to the chakra until it seems balanced.

Crystal Therapy - Ask the person to be healed to lay on a comfortable surface. The healer places crystals of the appropriate vibration around the chakra points to help balance those energies. Some healers use the same crystals for each healing; others meditate to get information about which crystals might be the most helpful in a particular case.

Charged Water Therapy - A crystal is placed in a glass of pure water and allowed to stand overnight. Use water from a clean stream, if you can obtain it, or bottled spring water. Some healers put the glass of pure water on a windowsill and put a piece of stained glass of an appropriate color between the glass and the window so that the rays of sunlight or moonlight must pass through the colored glass before hitting the water. The person then drinks the water. Another method is to charge the glass of water with white light by projecting a laser-like beam of energy into the glass as you hold it in your projective hand. Project this beam of light from the heart chakra, or use your intuition to direct you to use another chakra.

Breathing Color - The person to be healed visualizes strong color in his or her aura and then breathes in the color. Continue until you feel intuitively that the aura contains a preponderance of that color.

Aura Cleansing - Pass your hands through the aura of the person who wants to be healed. Visualize any negativity or energy blockages being pulled out as your hands move through the energetic bodies. When you sense that the aura is free of energy blockage, visualize pure color emanating from your projective hand and put it inside the aura as you pass your hands through the aura.

Absentee Healing - This therapy can be used whether the person to be healed is on the other side of the world or just across the street. Before you begin, request permission to do the healing. If you cannot request permission directly, allow your higher self to ask it of the other person's higher self. If you sense that the answer is "yes," visualize energy blockages being cleared from the aura and replace them with pure color or white light. If you sense that the answer is "no," then do not perform a healing. It will not work, because the person's higher self has indicated that a healing is not desired.

There are other methods that work equally well. Use whatever method works for you.

Using Healing Energy

In order to understand healing energy, the first thing you need to do is to discover what your own energy feels like and how to work with it.

These are the same steps you use when you actually perform a psychic healing. At this point, however, we just want to discover what our energy feels like and to get some feeling for how it works. As with any metaphysical activity, work with the process until you are sure about how and why it works.

▣ Relax, open your crown chakra, and bring in universal energy. Release tension, center, and ground yourself. If you are at all unsure of your abilities, ask your guides for their help.

▣ Hold your hands in front of you, palms facing toward each other about six inches apart, at chest height in front of your heart. There are minor chakras located in the center of the palms where the point of deepest indentation is when you hold your hands in a relaxed position. Begin to circulate the universal energy you bring in through the crown chakra down through one arm, out through one palm chakra and across the gap between the palms, into the other palm chakra, back up the other arm, and out one of your exhaust channels. When you feel that the energy is flowing strongly, bring your consciousness down into your heart center.

▣ Allow the energy to flow more strongly out into the gap between the hands and less strongly into the other palm so that it feels like excess energy is building up between the two hands. Slowly move your hands apart another six inches or so, and visualize that you are holding a ball between your hands. Allow the energy to build up even more. Then, when you have a feel for the energy that exists in the space between your hands, bring them back together again so that the space between is about half the size it was. You should be able to sense something being compressed between your hands. It might feel very much like you are pressing in on a volleyball. Compress and expand the energy until you have a feel for what it is like.

For now, do not worry too much about whether the energy you sense is real or just something you imagine. Remember, imagination is a *tool*. If you can sense the energy, accept that it really exists. Belief is an important component of psychic development. **You can do anything you believe you can do!**

In performing an actual healing, you will continue from this point. You may choose to work with either the astral or etheric body. If the person is available, begin by passing your hands through the appropriate energy body until it feels as though your hands are inside that body. It should feel the same to the person as well, since they know exactly where their various energy bodies exist. Change the location of your hands until the person feels that the location is appropriate, even if you were sure that you had it right. Remember, it is their energetic body you are working with, not yours, and they know where it is better than you do.

Continue passing your hands through their energetic bodies, allowing one hand (the **active** or **projective** hand) to channel universal energy into their energetic body and the other hand (the **passive** or **receptive** hand) to "vacuum" the negativity or dis-ease from them. Open your throat chakra and speak spontaneously as your hands process through their energy. You receive psychic impressions with your passive hand, and your throat chakra processes it and allows you to vocalize it as it passes upwards throughout your own energy fields. Do not edit as you speak - just say what occurs to you. Discharge the negative energy that you receive through your receptive hand by visualizing it streaming off the fingertips of that hand far out into space, into the sun, or into the center of the earth.

There are several points to remember:

☆ *Do not* heal others using your own energy. Remember to channel universal energy through you and through the subject in order to accomplish the healing.

☆ Also remember to discharge *everything* you pull in from the subject. Do not be naive and try to program yourself to retain anything positive you get from them or to assume that you can handle their energy. Some healers assume that anything positive they can get is worth seeking or they assume that they are "strong enough" to deal with any form of energy. You can get pure energy from the universe, so you do not need any from the subject, no matter how positive either of you think that energy is. Also, you are setting up a separate process whereby you require yourself to have to sort through energy and pick up what is positive while expending the negative, and that just complicates the purpose of the healing.

☆ Be sure to push the energy you absorb from the subject completely away from all of your energetic bodies. Visualizing it streaming out far into space accomplishes this easily and completely. I often visualize it being absorbed into a star, the sun, or a black hole in space.

Assuming that you are capable of dealing with anyone's energy is egotistical and is generally a false assumption. Why take the chance? **Always** channel away the energy you

Healing / 105

receive from those with whom you work and obtain universal energy for yourself when needed. Any small benefit you might receive from combining the two processes is far outweighed by the dangers.

Remember not to edit the information your throat chakra sends out. Just allow yourself to say whatever comes out of your mouth. Information that means nothing to you can make a great deal of sense to the subject.

You can practice psychic healing on your own aura, and your first attempts should be to heal yourself. You cannot heal others when your own aura is full of dense or negative vibrations. Healing yourself first will enable you to deal effectively and easily with others, and you will notice that the results you achieve will be far more substantial.

You may have trouble at first in discerning the different energies of the various energetic bodies. Try working with and attuning to crystals for the physical, plants for the etheric, and animals (such as a pet) for the astral. Involve all five physical senses as you work with energy.

12

Working With Color

One of the easiest ways to learn to manipulate energy is by associating it with color. The colors of the spectrum represent various vibrations of energy.

The easiest system is by associating color with the seven colors of the rainbow. In case you have forgotten your grade school lessons on rainbows (or if you have not seen one lately), here is a list of the colors of the rainbow in descending order of vibration:

☆ violet/purple

☆ indigo

☆ blue

☆ green

☆ yellow

☆ orange

☆ red

Since there are seven colors in a rainbow and seven major chakras, we can use this system to understand how chakras work by associating these colors with the seven chakras.

White is a combination of all colors. It is used to represent universal energy. When working psychically, note that the metaphysical concept of the color white is represented by a clear, colorless representation, rather like pure water, not like the whiteness of paint. The concept of clarity is of importance here. One cannot work psychically if the energy used is opaque like white paint; it would conceal rather than reveal. Be sure when working with **white light** and similar concepts that you are using clear colors, not opaque ones. Your visualizations of color should be similar to the colors found in stained glass rather than what is in a paint can. And make sure you visualize pure vibrant colors, not muddy representations.

Color Energies and Chakras

Using color is the fastest way to learn how chakra energy works. Here is a chart that illustrates how colors map to the seven major chakras and what that color vibration represents.

Chakra	Color	Vibration	Represents
1 Base	Blue	Physical Energy	Level of energy and awareness of the inner self
2 Navel	Orange	Emotional energy	
3 Solar Plexus	Yellow	Mental energy, thoughts	Inner knowledge
4 Heart	Green	Spiritual energy	Higher expression of feelings
5 Throat	Blue	Astral energy	Knowledge being transferred
6 Third Eye	Indigo	Etheric energy	Awareness in a higher spiritual framework of wisdom and understanding
7 Crown	Violet or Purple	Soul energy	Spiritual awareness
8 Spiritual	White	Universal energy	Enlightenment

Note: An eighth chakra, called the spiritual chakra, is described in the chart above. This chakra operates much like the crown chakra, but is located at the upper boundary of the spiritual energy body and encompasses the etheric, astral, mental, and spiritual bodies. This chakra is activated by communicating with the higher self, or with universal energy (that which has been called God, Goddess, All That Is, The Supreme Being, and so forth). Because the energy of this chakra is of such a fine vibration, it is difficult to access it consciously. However, it does exist and it works in the same way as the other chakras. By visualizing pure universal energy entering this chakra, we can probably cause something to happen in the same way that the other chakras respond to visualizations. Because of the level of vibration of this chakra, you will have little effect unless you can effectively work with the other chakras.

There are literally hundreds of ways to apply the energy of color to metaphysical work. Many books illustrate the use of various color systems. My advice is to try any of them that you feel attracted to and use those that work for you. Remember, there is no one way that works best for everyone.

Working with Color and Energy

Color is a visual representation of a particular vibration of energy. Because it is a representation of energy, color can be used as a tool to access that particular vibration.

The concept of positive and negative energies is an important one. Too much red in an accountant's aura can produce anger, hostility, and aggressiveness that would be unacceptable in that environment and it can be considered a negative energy. However, a boxer who energizes his aura with red produces anger, hostility, and aggressiveness that will probably be very effective in the ring. For the boxer, it is a positive use of the energy. It is not the color in itself that is positive or negative, it is the *application* of that color in an aura that connotes positivity or negativity.

The following chart illustrates some of the traditional metaphysical uses of color.

Color	Aspects
Gold	Love and compassion. Foundation of consciousness. Corresponds to keywords: positive, sun, light, masculine, warmth, creative
Silver	Detachment, higher sources of knowing. Color of the astral cord; connection to essence. Corresponds to keywords: negative, moon, reflective, feminine, cool, regenerative.
Purple	Spiritual power. Imagination. Mastery. Tests what is real.
Lavender	Balance, harmony, integration of all aspects of being.
Blue	Clarity. Peace. Creative self-expression. Authority. Calming, cleansing. Nurturing. Mentality. Healing. Increases intuition.
Red	Physical energy and vitality, physical power. Demands attention. Stimulates passion, appetite, violence, anger and hostility, aggression.
Pink	Personal/self love. Calming. Serenity.
Orange	Intuition and emotional vitality. Sexuality.
Yellow	Intellect, conscious mind. Learning. Energy.

Color	Aspects
Green	Healing for physical body (except cancers and unhealthy growths). Growth. Physical balance.
Brown	Grounding, eliminating. Confusion.
White	Purity. All colors are contained in white, so it is a substitute for any other color. Protect, heal, energize, purify. Divine love.
Black	Magnetic, draws light and energy to itself. Highly attractive. Absorbs light. Gravity, loss of power. Invisibility. The Void.

Note: Metaphysically, black is considered to be a color and it has enormous power. The color black is created when no other colors exist, or, to put it another way, in the absence of the energy of the other colors. Black exists in a state of nothingness that in metaphysics is called **the void.** The void is a state of great potential, because *anything* can replace *nothing.* Do not consider black a negative color simply because it is black. Used correctly, it has enormous benefit and can produce an unbelievable amount of positive energy. Used incorrectly, or for the wrong purposes, it is dangerous. Before using black in a visualization, it is an excellent idea to know what you are doing and how energy works. Be very sure of your intent when using black metaphysically. It is a good idea to try using other colors first and resorting to black when these attempts do not accomplish what you want.

Energizing the Aura with Color

Using the chart above that shows the correpondences between colors and energy, you can energize your aura to produce certain effects. This is the easiest way that I know of to make significant change in your life. It takes only a few moments of quiet time and a bit of concentration to produce tremendous benefit.

Remember to visualize strong, transparent, glowing colors. The colors you visualize should resemble the colors seen in stained glass, not in paint. Do not choose washed out or muddy colors. Choose strong, assertive colors that positively glow with energy as you see them in your mind's eye.

Color for the Imagination Impaired

If you are not a visual person - for example, you have problems seeing in your mind's eye how your new furniture will fit into your living room, or if you are uncertain about choosing paint colors - do not be discouraged. You can work with color! One easy method is to buy the largest box of crayons you can get. From the box, choose the color you feel is the closest match to the energy of what is needed in the visualization. On a clean piece of white paper, scribble with the crayon, leaving the tip on the paper the entire time and make swirls or circles as you follow the same visualization presented in the exercise. Having a physical representation of color in front of you allows you to access that energy. Even though I think this is a good way to fool the conscious mind, remember that whether or not your conscious mind thinks you can, your energetic bodies can do the exercise and *can* work effectively with color!

Color Exercise

 At the edge of your aura directly above your head, visualize a pair of doors opening inward. Visualize a bright white light streaming down into this opening, changing into brilliant color just before it enters your aura. Let the color swirl down into your aura, filling the space and glowing with energy. The sensation might feel like you are a balloon being filled with water or like a hurricane wind gusting around you. Feel it swirling around as it permeates into every part of your physical self. Any energy blockages or negativity are blasted away as this powerful color moves throughout your being. You might feel as if you are standing in a strong wind.

 Allow the color to completely fill your aura, until no more color can enter. At this point, close the opening in your aura, continuing to allow the color to swirl around in your aura for a few minutes more. If, during this time, you sense any negativity or blockages, visualize them as being surrounded by the same brilliant color you are using, and send them down into the ground below you and far into the earth. You can also visualize these blockages as being sent directly into the sun that consumes them completely.

When you feel energized, end the visualization. Remember that the color in your aura will last for many hours, sometimes even days or weeks. When you feel as if it is no longer there, just perform the visualization again.

You can use either one specific color or a rainbow of colors. Choose whichever feels appropriate to you.

13

Psychic Readings

Everyone is psychic. Some people choose to develop that ability. With that in mind, it follows that anyone can learn to receive psychic impressions and, therefore, give **psychic readings.** You can choose to go to another person for a reading or you can perform them yourself.

One inherent problem in trying to perform a psychic reading for yourself is that you will probably find that you are less accurate when reading for yourself than when you do a reading for others. This is because you are in the middle of living your own life. It is difficult to gain perspective while you're trying to get through a situation. Other readers are not dealing with these issues and can give a less biased reading.

First let's look at what to expect when consulting someone else for a psychic reading.

Receiving a Psychic Reading

Different people need different kinds of readings. Somewhere out there, you can find a psychic who can provide exactly the kind of reading you need. To find someone appropriate for you, it helps to ask around, and you will probably have to suffer through a few unsuccessful readings before you are able to find a reader with whom you feel comfortable.

Choose a psychic with whom you sense some rapport. If the person annoys you in any way, you are less likely to receive a good reading from them because of the passive resistance you have to overcome before you begin.

Avoid, if you can, the stereotypical "psychic" who has a storefront operation. Also avoid those who adopt a bizarre persona in order to make you feel like you are consulting someone special. I know dozens of good psychics. I also know a lot of so-called psychics who have no concept of what being psychic really is. Their function is to amuse the world-weary and to part them from some of their cash. Ask your friends if they know anyone that they can recommend. The goal, of course, is to find a psychic who can channel appropriate information for your life.

Ask if the psychic has a professional background in doing psychic readings. Also ask about their training. You'll find almost every psychic has been self-trained, primarily because until recently there were few classes offered to help with psychic development.

When booking your appointment, ask the following questions:

☆ Clarify what you are looking for and ask if the psychic feels you can work together.

☆ Ask for recommendations if you think that would be helpful. Each psychic works differently.

☆ Learn about the process your psychic uses. If the psychic cannot define how he or she works, then there is little guarantee that she knows how to access information for you. There is no secret formula that cannot be divulged. Psychics who make a mystery out of what they do are usually less accurate than those who know what they are doing and can express how it works to you.

☆ Psychic Fairs are often good sources if you are looking for someone new and they are generally inexpensive. You can get a trial reading at a Fair and pay only a few dollars; consulting the psychic directly is likely to cost you much more.

☆ Be wary of television or radio psychics. Although many very good psychics do radio shows, I know of some shows that were rigged by allowing only callers who are known by the psychic to get on the air. However, the short reading (five minutes or less, usually) is free if you can get on the air. Try it and take the information received with the proverbial grain of salt. If it applies to you and is accurate, perhaps you have found an appropriate psychic.

☆ Ask how long the session will last.

☆ Ask about the fee. Reputable psychics state their fee up front and generally it is not open for negotiation. Avoid any psychic who will not quote a firm fee based on a session of a specified length, or those who request "love offerings." If the psychic does not know what his services are worth, there is no reason why you should make that determination instead.

During the reading, avoid questions that can generate yes/no answers. *Yes* and *no* are words that imply that you are asking permission. You are not consulting your parents;

you are asking a psychic a question and your goal is to get an answer that supplies some details that allow you to make your own decision and determine a course of action that is appropriate for your situation.

Organize yourself before you leave for the reading. Assemble your questions in advance and write them down if you have less than a perfect memory. It is difficult to remember them during a session. Ask in advance if you can bring a tape recorder, and be sure to bring a spare tape. Also, test the recorder just before you leave for the reading. I cannot begin to calculate how many times while doing a reading I have had to wait because the tape recorder's batteries have gone dead or because the person spends fifteen minutes rummaging through the trunk of the car before recalling that the tape is back home on the kitchen table. If you cannot arrive prepared and attentive, then reschedule the appointment.

Some psychics do not allow the reading to be tape recorded. Many of the eastern states have antiquated laws about psychic readings. Some readers do not allow taping as a precaution against being prosecuted for doing readings. If that is the case, they are not likely to change their mind. Bring a pad of paper and a couple of pens, and take copious notes instead.

Arrive on time. Many psychics schedule several appointments each day and a latecomer can upset a schedule for an entire day. The fee that you are charged represents a certain block of time that the psychic is willing to give you. If you arrive late, the reading will very likely still end at the same time as originally agreed. I guarantee that it will not be cheaper than previously agreed.

If you are dealing with a reputable professional psychic, your reading will probably be enjoyable and informative. However, there are disreputable people posing as psychics. Following is a list of fraudulent practices used by disreputable psychics. Run, do not walk, from these people whenever one of the following is noted:

- You are told that someone has put a curse on you, but that this psychic can remove it for a fee. The fee is always just about what this con artist thinks you can pay. It starts high and is negotiated downwards until you agree to it. Leave immediately. File a complaint with the police.

- You are told not to discuss the reading with anybody because it will affect the outcome. If the psychic is receiving accurate information, discussing it with others will not have any effect on it.

- Your reading consists of gross generalizations that flatter you but give you no useful information.

- Your reader can only give you past life information.

- Your reader can only give you predictions about the future, but cannot shed light on why these things might happen to you.

- Your reader asks more questions than you do. While reputable readers ask for clarification, they will not expect you to provide them with any personal information, and you will not hear this information repeated to you during the reading as "new" information.

- The fee changes from what was quoted when you made your appointment - unless you use more time than you were allocated. Anyone who has to answer questions for an hour deserves more money than if they were doing it for half an hour. If you were told that a half hour reading was $30 and you stayed an hour, you should not be surprised that the fee for your reading is $60.

☆ The reader acts mysterious or strange, uses mumbo-jumbo, or supplies cryptic messages. If you do not understand what is being discussed, then you are not getting a valid reading.

☆ The reader mentions Satan, the devil, or that there are evil influences on your life.

☆ The psychic tries to convince you of something that you do not believe in.

☆ The psychic tries to convince you to do something you are not comfortable with. A reputable psychic understands that it is ultimately *your* decision to make changes in your life.

☆ The reader tries to tell you that you are wrong and he or she is right, regardless of the topic.

☆ The reader belittles other psychics.

By consulting only the most reputable psychics, you are assuring yourself of an evidential, reliable reading. Why would you want to settle for anything less than that?

Performing a Psychic Reading

The first steps, as usual, are to relax, center, and ground yourself.

After you relax all of your muscles, allow your energy to center and move into place, and disperse any excess energy into the earth, you will be physically able to receive psychic impressions. Begin to visualize your energy increasing in vibration as you open your crown chakra to allow clean, pure universal energy to pour into your aura.

When you feel that your energy has increased in vibration, open your solar plexus chakra. Next, open your base chakra. This will improve your receptivity of physical world evidence. Open the throat chakra next to ensure clear communication of the impressions that you receive. The last chakra opened is the heart chakra. This brings a spiritual energy to the reading and brings in the energy of universal love which ensures that whatever you say will be received as helpful information. This reflects your intentions in doing a reading. You are not there to be judgmental and critical.

Pay attention to the person whom you are reading. If you notice that the person is leaning away from you or frowning, try opening your heart chakra a little bit more to see if that improves the situation. (You open the heart chakra by sensing the other person's value and realizing that you are going to gain something from the interchange of information and energy.) If the person appears to be at ease, you are probably getting accurate and helpful information. However, do not edit the information to satisfy the person! That someone is smiling comfortably at you means that they are receptive to your information, but not that it is correct!

Your intention when doing readings is to receive correct information. Do not allow the person to consult you to confirm their misinformation. If that is what is happening, do not allow their intention to manipulate the information into confirmation of whatever it is that they want to hear to interfere with your purpose. Thankfully, this type of manipulation is often blatantly obvious and your ethical behavior will be challenged more than once as your higher self weighs and gauges your growth.

As information begins to pour into your aura, relax your mind and allow whatever you receive to float up from the solar plexus into your consciousness. At this point, my advice is to forget the chakras and concentrate instead on doing a reading. The chakras will take care of themselves as they always do! Consider the information you receive as if it were water in a pipe. If you allow water to flow through a pipe, more water follows. If you stop the flow, there is no room for any more water to move into the pipe. Halting the flow of information is called **blocking**. You can either perform a psychic reading or you can block the reception of information, but you can only do one at a time.

Start talking to the subject, describing whatever you are receiving in whatever way seems appropriate. Information is nothing more than energy and it is released by expressing it. Information withheld has no value to either of you. Even if it feels completely wrong, you will not be able to get anything else because the space is already occupied. Do not worry about how the information is being received unless you are obviously distressing the subject. Just keep talking. Notice that you are talking in terms of what you *sense* rather than what you *think*.

Do not *edit* the information you receive! What has little or no meaning to you might very well be meaningful to the person you are reading. If you think before you speak, you can change the information in some small way. If the person tells you that the information you are receiving has no meaning to him or her, let it go and move on to another topic. Nobody receives information that is one hundred percent accurate. The problem is, you have lived *your* life and that is the filter for *all* information you receive.

Another aspect of editing the information you receive is when you get wrong impressions. Sometimes your own ego sends you information about yourself; it is not dead, after all! In most other cases, you have simply misinterpreted what you received. The only way you will learn to tell the difference between valid psychic impressions and "other information," whatever that may be, is to get the wrong information to begin with. You have to have something to compare. It is a natural process of learning. If you know how to type, for example, you probably remember pressing a lot of wrong keys when you began learning! It works the same way with psychic readings.

If you are not receiving anything, be wary of the human tendency to strain for results. You will notice a muscular tightening somewhere in the body, and that is a good sign that you are pushing to receive an impression. If you tighten your muscles, you block the transfer of energy, and you end up getting nothing. This often happens to beginning psychics.

No psychic can read for everyone. If you find you are not receiving anything and no readjustment seems to work, give up. Admitting that you are not receiving information is not the same as admitting defeat. The quality of your abilities is not at stake. This is not an area where you have to prove yourself. Allow yourself to have limitations, whatever they are!

Methods for Receiving Psychic Information

There are probably as many methods for receiving psychic impressions as there are people in the world. Here are some of the more common methods:

Psychometry - the divination of facts about an object or its owner by touching or viewing the object. Photographs and jewelry are frequently used.

Runes - small flat stones inscribed with letters of the ancient Viking alphabet. Each letter corresponds to a condition or philosophy of life which can be interpreted as having an influence on the person's life.

Astrology/horoscopes - the analysis of human character and the prediction of events by the position and aspects of the planets. A natal chart which describes the correlation of planets at the time, date, and place of birth is used to determine influences that might affect the person's life. Astrology deals with *possibilities*, not with a preordained future.

Dream interpretation - the use of the symbology of dreams to obtain insight for self development. A series of dreams can be recorded in a dream journal for later interpretation. **Lucid dreaming** is the use of dream images that are received in a conscious, aware state. "People can be fully conscious while remaining asleep and dreaming at the same time." *(Lucid Dreaming*, Stephen LaBerge, page xi. Ballantine Books, 1985.)

Tarot card reading - the use of a special deck of cards containing 78 images and divided into two groups. The Major Arcana contains 56 cards; the Minor Arcana contains 22 cards. Each card describes certain aspects of life. Used together in a reading, these powerful symbols tell a story. They can be used to divine the future, to analyze or evaluate personal experience, or to work with archetypes.

I-ching - an ancient Chinese system of divination that uses 64 patterns called hexagrams. Originally the hexagrams were drawn on sticks of yarrow; today specially marked coins are often substituted.

Numerology - a system that assigns a specific vibration to numbers. The alphabetic characters in a name are translated to numbers and added, or the date of birth is added, and the sum is used to correlate with a chart of influences.

Channelling/trance channelling - the current term for what used to be called mediumship. Channellers allow their voice or body to be used by discarnate or nonhuman entities who want to communicate, teach, guide, or otherwise interact with humans. Channelling can be done fully consciously, but more often, a channeller uses a lightly hypnotic trance state in order to reduce the chance of conscious thought interrupting the flow of information from other dimensions.

Palmistry - the practice of reading a person's character or future using the marks on the palms of the hand. The left hand describes influences at birth; the right hand illustrates how the possibilities shown on the left hand have been realized during the person's life.

Automatic writing - the ability to channel information from spirit guides or nonhuman entities by writing without conscious control.

Handwriting analysis - an analysis of a person's character using the peculiarities of their handwriting. Since no two people have the same handwriting, subtle clues about character can be discerned by close observation of the graphic nature of their writing and applying general theories of various character traits extrapolated from the study of thousands of other people who write in a similar way. Also called **graphology**.

Kirlian photography - a photographic process developed by Russian electrician Semyon Kirlian and his wife that captures the color patterns of an aura (human or plant). It was used originally to diagnose illness. Some analysts of kirlian photographs can read past life information from the photographs. A film is laid on a plate and the object to be photographed is pressed onto the plate while a current of electricity of 75,000 to 200,000 pulses per second runs through it. Occasionally you will be able to find someone with a Kirlian camera at psychic fairs or new age expositions who will take a photograph of you and then interpret it. Since they are usually located in a public area of the fair or expo, stand near the booth for a few minutes and listen to the readings. If they tend to be filled with platitudes and non-information, do not bother having a reading. Just because someone has high tech equipment does not mean they have any psychic ability. Make sure you get what you pay for.

Biorhythms - a method of equating physical, emotional, and mental fluctuations. The physical cycle is 23 days; the emotional cycle is 28 days; and the mental cycle is 33 days long. Various activities are either difficult or easy to accomplish depending on when they occur during these cycles.

Pendulum dowsing - a method of determining "yes" or "no" responses to questions. A small object is attached to a string or fine chain and held steadily while the question is asked. The object will begin to move clockwise (generally a "yes" answer) or counterclockwise (a "no" answer). However, each person is different, so a dowser usually asks a question to which the answer is already known, and bases the correlation of clockwise/counterclockwise direction on that response. **Dowsing** can be done with a bent stick or bent metal rods and is often used to find underground water supplies. Dowsers can also find **ley lines**, which are a pathway of electrical forces believed to be generated by the life force of the Earth itself. A grid of ley lines has been acknowledged for thousands of years in locations all over the earth. There is a strong ley line in southern England that has been acknowledged for hundreds of years. It is clearly marked and easily accessible, and stretches from St Michael's Mount at the southwestern tip of the country, passes through several power spots, including Glastonbury and Stonehenge, and ends near London. Other well known and well marked ley lines can be found around Sedona, Arizona and on the Hawaiian islands.

Psychic drawing - similar to automatic writing, but instead of writing words and sentences, the result is a line drawing.

Tea leaves - the art of interpreting the meaning of the patterns of tea leaves that are left in the bottom of the cup. The tea must be made with loose tea and the person drinks the tea before the reading.

Past life regression - the process of accessing the soul's memory of former lives by using guided meditation.

Mediumship/spirit guides - a channelling method that uses the interaction with spirit guides to discern answers about the life path or concerns about the future.

Aura readings - the interpretation of colors surrounding the physical bodies. These colors are visual representations of the energies of the subtle bodies. Aura readings are used for past life regressions, predicting the future, and general questions about health.

Scrying - also called crystal gazing. A round sphere of quartz crystal is used to focus and deepen intuition. Clairvoyant images can be seen if the eyes are slightly unfocused and are gazing at a point near the center of the ball. Use quartz crystal for best results, even if you can afford only a small sphere. Using lead crystal (glass) is not as effective, although it does work.

How the Tools Work

No matter what method you choose to employ, you can get valid results. All methods, however, use at least one of three basic techniques: clairvoyance, clairaudience, or clairsentience. These are often called the **psychic senses** or **"the sixth sense."**

Clairvoyance means *clear seeing*. The third eye chakra receives visual impressions. In early stages of development, these are often symbolic images or **archetypes**. Archetypes are symbolic representations for universal concepts. In later stages of development, you can see more pictorial representations which reflect the person's physical reality. These images are fleeting, difficult to grasp and to remember even moments after receiving them.

Clairvoyance can be developed, although many people never receive visual impressions regardless of how hard they try. If you can look at an empty room and visualize whether your furniture will fit and how it will look, you are probably visually-oriented and might be able to develop clairvoyance. Clairvoyant images are not the same as visual images in the physical world; once you have experienced clairvoyant sight, you will see that it is easy to distinguish between the two types of visual images.

Clairaudience means *clear hearing*. The crown chakra receives audible impressions. These impressions can sound like physical voices or like synthesized speech. Some clairaudients can receive vocal impressions of their guides. This ability is one that is usually *not* developed because it is difficult to turn it off once you learn how it works. Mental institutions are full of people who are probably not insane, but merely clairaudient.

Clairsentience means *clear knowing* or *clear sensing.* The solar plexus chakra receives information that it sends out to the conscious mind. Most people are clairsentient rather than clairaudient or clairvoyant. It is far easier to develop this ability than clairvoyance because your expectations do not work against you. Most people have expectations about what clairvoyance is (for example, expecting a clairvoyant image to appear the same as visual images in the physical world). As with any preconceived notion, if the ability does not develop according to that concept, the energy gets blocked because it is "not right." Because this sense operates through the solar plexus, which is located just below the breastbone and very close to the stomach, it is often called "gut instinct" or "gut feeling." Exercising this ability means that you will just know some fact without having gotten the information through your physical five senses.

However information comes to you, allow yourself to receive it. There is no intrinsic value in being clairvoyant over being clairsentient. Many people are fascinated by clairvoyance, for example, because that ability has been portrayed dozens of times in B-grade movies. Movies are a visual medium, as is clairvoyance, so it is easy to portray the two concepts in the same way. Just remember that all of these methods work equally well. Your higher self already knows best how you can receive psychic information. Trying to change how that way works for you will only block the transmission of energy.

14

Channelling

Channelling is the same process that used to be known as *spiritual mediumship*. Many of the mediums who practiced around the turn of the last century were proven to be frauds and the term *medium* went out of favor. Because of that the term *channeller* is now used. But, channeller or medium, the process is exactly the same.

Rather than being just a process whereby one receives psychic impressions, channellers acknowledge that there are not only other states of consciousness, but also other conscious lifeforms, called **entities**, that exist in the universe. These entities can be earthbound discarnates, astral entities, highly evolved spiritual beings who exist in spirit rather than physical form, and even angels. Channellers focus on the evolved beings (often called **guides**) because the information received from them has far greater value. Frequently the physical world incarnational paths of these beings either is complete or more likely they never existed physically at all. A **discarnate being** (a human who has recently died, usually) has no more knowledge in the etheric or astral planes where it now exists than the person had before death. **Lower astral entities** have little of value to offer; they are attracted by negativity of any kind and do not have the exposure to the types of knowledge that you are seeking. Very often they are nothing more than powerful thoughtforms, composed of energy but containing no intelligence. **Thoughtforms** are energy robots and can only provide information that has been built into them during their construction. Generally, such information is useless for any purpose other than what it was programmed for.

When learning how to channel, it is extremely important to focus from the first effort on seeking information *only* from evolved beings. You can get information from discarnates or lower astral entities using other means - the Ouija board is a notorious example - but since the information has no real value, you will gain little from it. Putting the same amount of energy towards seeking information and enlightenment from evolved beings is evidence of your own spiritual level. Energy is attracted to its own vibration. If you seek a higher vibration, your own vibration will rise. If you amuse yourself with information from the lower vibrations, your own vibration will lower. Remember that your vibration is nothing more than a reflection of the quality of your life.

The term **trance channelling** might need some explanation. Trance is a form of an altered state of mind and can be easily induced by using some form of hypnosis. Drugs also induce altered states but your vibration is severely lowered using that form of trance because the drug affects the physical body. Hypnotic trance significantly raises the vibration. Some channellers are light trance subjects, which means they are aware of the information that they are transmitting; others are medium trance subjects, which means that much less of their personality is apt to be involved and that they will have less recall of what has transpired; and a very few are deep trance subjects who retain nothing of what has occurred. Deep trance channellers are relatively rare: about 70% of the world's population can be hypnotized and less than 10% of that group have deep trance abilities.

Light and medium trance subjects, however, are quite common, so most people can learn how to hypnotize themselves.

The ability to channel takes a lot of effort, concentration, and resolve. It involves learning as much as possible about yourself, because until you can identify your own energy and understand why it is there, you cannot locate another being who exists as energy. Some people are natural channellers because that is part of what they chose to accomplish in this lifetime, but even those people will have difficulty unless they have learned to focus, relax, center, ground, and live ethically.

How Channelling Works

It is usually easier to channel with your eyes closed. Eliminate as much physical world distraction as you can.

You do not need to achieve a deep trance to be able to channel your guides. A light hypnotic trance - similar to the state you are in when you daydream - works just as well. Before you begin, reaffirm to yourself that you intend to channel only the highest level guide you can receive. This is a practical way to eliminate the discarnates, thought-forms, and other lower astral entities that might decide to communicate with you while you are in your receptive meditative state. You will receive only the type of guide and the level of information that you choose.

There is no need to worry about being possessed by the entity you channel. You are receiving information in the same way that a radio receives information. Your initial affirmation to channel only the highest level guide you can receive is like setting your radio tuner on a specific channel (or in this case, a range of channels). Once you have channelled a particular guide, your tuner becomes set to that particular vibration and it becomes easier to locate that entity and receive information.

Channelling Exercise - Meeting Your Guide

▧ Sit comfortably in a quiet room. As usual, take the phone off the hook, put the dog outside, and send the kids to the mall.

▧ Either verbally or mentally, affirm that you will receive only the highest vibration available. Since there are always representatives of the higher realms available to you, you will not attract a lower astral entity as long as you make your intentions clear. If, after beginning, you do not feel comfortable with the information you are receiving, just stop channelling and try again another time, remembering to reaffirm that you are always seeking *only* the highest vibration available to you.

▧ Visualize white light entering your aura from the opened crown chakra. Allow this light to swirl about inside your aura and remove any blockages, physical discomfort or pain, or emotional trauma found there. Send the excess energy out through the bottoms of the feet, or if you are sitting down, through the bottom of the spine, deeply into the earth.

Although I strongly discourage the use of props, soft music, candles, or incense, they can help raise the vibration while you are practicing how to channel. They are tools; it is important not to become so addicted to their presence that you cannot do any psychic work without them. You need to learn to be receptive and aware anywhere in the world, under any conditions.

- As you sit quietly, begin to feel the calm, loving presence of your guides as these entities draw near. They will make their presence known in their own time. Just be open to their arrival and to whatever information you sense as you sit and meditate.

- Verbally or mentally ask your guides for help. Tell them why you want to channel and what you hope to accomplish. You can make contact only if your intentions are strong and focused.

Several attempts in which you ask only one or two questions are preferable to a long session. If you have not channelled before, you might find it physically tiring, because it is difficult to sit in any one position for any length of time. Once you have contacted a guide, it becomes easier to do it again.

- After asking your question, sit quietly and enjoy your guide's company. Being in the presence of a guide often feels like sitting and talking with a loving old friend. It is refreshing, invigorating, and soothing all at the same time.

- After a few moments, thank your guide for helping you and return to waking consciousness. If you have trouble opening your eyes, just wiggle a toe or make a small physical movement.

When you have finished, be sure to write your observations in a journal. These impressions, like any received in an altered state, are ephemeral and quickly lost.

15

Crystals

There are five important **kingdoms** acknowledged to exist in the metaphysical world. The spiritual kingdom is the highest vibration, followed by humans, animals, plants, and finally minerals. The inhabitants of each of these kingdoms possess a consciousness and a vibration of a particular range. In the mineral kingdom, **crystals** are the most evolved form of mineral consciousness.

The amount of movement of which the participants of a specific kingdom are capable is an indicator of vibrational levels. In the physical world, humans are the least restricted in movement and, in fact, have invented machines to help them move about the entire world. Animals are also quite unrestricted in movement, but if they need assistance, they generally use each other rather than machines and usually only move about on a particular continent. Plants move significantly less; once rooted, they generally stay in that place for an entire existence. Their focus on movement is in transporting seeds so that their offspring can experience life in a different place. Minerals do not move about much at all, and what little movement does take place happens over periods of, perhaps, thousands of years. Their movement is usually initiated by other kingdoms because of phenomena in the physical world such as drought, flood, lack of food, change in climate, and so forth.

This means that minerals can teach us about qualities like patience, endurance, solidity, and so forth. Most crystals are formed underground, so their exposure to the physical realm is limited. However, they are formed by a slow but steady interaction between water and the earth's surface minerals. Water is an excellent storage vehicle for information and energy, which are imbued in crystals. It is said that crystals form when the mineral kingdom has accumulated a significant body of information, carried by water, and that the crystals thus formed are later liberated and brought into contact with the human kingdom in order to pass along this information.

It is believed that crystals are formed quickly, often in a matter of minutes. An enormous amount of energy is required to form a crystal. Much of that energy remains with the crystal after formation. Energy stores information and moves it around, and these are the two primary uses of a crystal: to either transmit information or to move energy.

These members of the mineral kingdom are *tools* designed to help with our growth. There is, as I have said before, no intrinsic value in a rock. It will not magically deliver information to you on its own. It is like holding a battery. Although there is energy available from it, it is accessible only by certain methods. Just as you do not feel an electrical shock each time you pick up a battery, you will not get a blast of psychic information each time you handle a crystal. Working with crystals requires concentration, a strong focus of attention and energy, and a good idea about how energy works. Crystals serve as a focal point and allow us to work with energy by amplifying our intentions and desires.

When working with crystals, open the base chakra. This chakra connects us to the earth plane energy, and the same energy that is contained in the crystal is constantly accessed through this chakra. The process of opening the base chakra and aligning with the mineral kingdom to produce stability is called **grounding**. Grounding is required in any attempt to receive psychic information.

When you receive a crystal, its energy can be temporarily distorted because of the environments through which it has passed. Many of you will be drawn to the wonderful soft yet powerful energy of clear quartz crystals. I think their energy is amazing, considering the way they have been treated before you acquire them.

Most crystals are mined in third world countries. Workers crawl into tunnels only a few feet high, sometimes slithering a half mile or more into the earth. These workers are often children six, seven, or eight years old. They earn only pennies a day and their work day is typically ten or twelve hours long. Needless to say, their lives are not very joyful. It is likely that some of the gloom they feel is transmitted into the stones as they lie among them. The stones are crudely cracked out of their matrix with sledgehammers and picks and thrown into large iron hoppers that move on railroad tracks to remove them from the mine. When the car stops, they are dumped into vats containing strong acid and boiled for several days. They are then moved into warehouses where they are broken into smaller pieces; dealers buy them by the ton after haggling over the price. When they arrive in this country, other dealers haggle over them in a series of sales until they arrive at your local shop. If this was your history, how would you feel?

Crystal Attunement Exercise

Before you begin working with crystals, take a moment to attune to the crystal that you have chosen. Sit comfortably in a quiet place; center and ground yourself. Hold the crystal in your receptive hand. Notice the images you receive. Sometimes they are historical: brief glimpses from the crystal about its history. Occasionally you can receive cosmic insight as soon as you begin working with the crystal, but do not expect this to happen. Instead, allow the energy within the crystal to work with your own energy. Most often, this energy can be translated as emotion: sadness, joy, peacefulness. A crystal that transmits anything other than joyfulness and peacefulness needs to be carefully cleared.

Working With Crystals

There are four processes to follow to work effectively with crystals:

☆ Choosing

☆ Clearing

☆ Charging

☆ Caring

Choosing a crystal is often the most enjoyable part of the experience. As more and more people begin to work with crystals, they are becoming easier to find and the prices are going down. You can often get a three inch clear quartz crystal in excellent condition (no broken tips or facets) for less than $5.00. Your crystal does not have to be in perfect condition in order for you to work well with it. Shop around a bit and get the nicest one you can afford. As you shop, hold the crystals that appeal to you visually in your receptive hand. Mentally ask yourself if this crystal is one with which you can work well. The crystals that draw your eye and attract you are good possibilities. It is interesting to notice how, in a box of two dozen crystals that are very much alike, you will be drawn to two or three. This procedure helps you to access your intuitive abilities.

Keeping their history in mind, it is important to realize that psychically they can be in sad shape as they lie there glittering in the showcase. They need to be cleared. **Clearing** involves visualizing the negativity flowing out of the stones, transmuting into positive energy, and then flowing deeply into the earth back to the mines to alleviate the suffering and disharmony there. This process can take moments or weeks, depending on their history, and it cannot be rushed. Some crystal dealers routinely clear their stones before offering them for sale. Many dealers do this not because it is good for the crystal, but because it is good for their business. People are more attracted to - and will buy - stones that are cleared. If in doubt, clear the crystal yourself. I make it a rule always to clear newly acquired stones. It can't hurt, and it is an opportunity for you to align with their energy as you work with them. Any opportunity you get to work with your intuition is one that you should take advantage of!

After clearing a crystal, it needs to be charged. **Charging** it with energy returns some of the life force that was lost in the journey from the mine to you. The easiest method for doing this is to hold it in your projective hand and to visualize universal energy streaming into it. You can work with one crystal or several at the same time. Visualize colored energy if it feels appropriate; white light is always acceptable. Picture the energy as a laser beam and really blast them! Another method is to expose them to the rays of the moon or sun. Use the moon's energy for receptive projects and the sun's energy for projective tasks. You can also put them near **generator crystals** to absorb that energy. Generator crystals are large clear quartz crystals that have been cleared and highly charged with positive energy. After charging them, you can begin to work with the stones.

Remember occasionally to **care** for them by washing them in mildly soapy water and rinsing them well. This removes dirt, dust, and oils left on them by your fingers and allows their energy to flow freely. A mild solution of dishwashing soap is ideal for cleaning crystals. Avoid chemical cleansers. Be sure to rinse them well to eliminate any soap residue that will attract dust particles to adhere to the crystal.

Crystals can either be used **receptively**, which means you channel universal energy in to yourself through them, or **projectively**, which means that you send out your energy through them in order to accomplish a specific goal. Specific types of crystals are used for specific purposes. There is a general list of these uses in the appendix; you can refer to one of the books on crystals for more detailed information.

There is a metaphysical philosophy that says that you do not *own* a crystal; you are merely serving as its guardian. As you work with crystals, you will find that an appropriate stone will manifest itself into your life at the proper time. At one time, I wanted to experiment with an Aqua Aura. This is a clear quartz crystal that has been coated with a very thin layer of gold and then put in a furnace and baked at a very high temperature. The gold bonds chemically with the clear crystal and turns a beautiful deep shade of celestial blue after this treatment. Because of the high price of gold, Aqua Aura is not cheap, and I could not find a suitable one anywhere. While looking at a display of crystals in a store one day, the owner handed me a small dish and asked me to put it on a nearby table. It was filled with small and very affordable Aqua Aura crystals!

It is also interesting to note that often when someone you know mentions needing a crystal for a particular purpose, it seems that you have just the stone. Pass it along if it feels right. A tool that is not used is worthless. The only way crystals can move about in the physical world is by relying on their human guardians.

Elementals

Elementals are nature spirits who inhabit each of the four elements:

Elementals	Element
Gnomes	Earth
Undines	Water
Sylphs	Air
Salamanders	Fire

These spirits were visible to people of earlier times who lived in close communion with nature. Work with undines when you are working with emotion; with sylphs when you are working with mentality or thought; and with salamanders for increasing energy. Work with gnomes when you want to manifest something, or any time you work with crystals, since these are the elemental energies of the crystal itself.

If often helps to do a little research and to find illustrations of how these various elementals have appeared to others in the past. Using the same appearance when you visualize can help you to connect to their energy. There are usually several different forms of the same elemental; for example, gnomes can also appear as fairies, pixies, dwarves, or elves.

In performing the crystal visualization exercise, you will encounter a gnome. These entities have enormous knowledge about their own realms that can be helpful to you as you study and work with alternate realities. Many years ago, a group of people settled in Findhorn (pronounced finned-horn) in Scotland and began to plant elaborate gardens. As they planted, they communicated with plant elementals who told them what the plants needed in order to survive in the harsh climate and very poor soil conditions that exist in that part of Scotland.

Their gardens would not have survived if they had planted under normal conditions using only their previous knowledge of gardening.

Crystal Visualization Exercise

This visualization exercise can help you attune to the energy of crystals. A clear quartz crystal often works best for this visualization if you are trying to work with crystals for the first time, but you can use any crystal to which you are attuned.

▣ Sit or lie in a comfortable position and breathe rhythmically. Hold your crystal in your receptive hand. Consciously relax as you breathe. Bring energy in as you inhale, hold it briefly while experiencing it in all of your body, and then expel the excess energy as you breathe out.

▣ As you begin to feel tranquil and relaxed, visualize your crystal changing from solid to a more fluid form.

Feel yourself becoming smaller and smaller as this occurs, until you are much smaller than the crystal you are holding. One of the facets will open slowly towards you, allowing you to enter.

▣ Stop and observe your surroundings. The air is cool, clear, and crisp, and the atmosphere is alive with tiny sparks of energy. Look around you. Look upwards and watch light enter the crystal and see it change into colors that swirl about and drift downwards to where you stand. Eventually these colors will envelop you with every color of the rainbow. Allow this colored energy to circulate within yourself and feel it remove any vestiges of tension and disharmony. Stay within this cleansing force until you feel completely refreshed.

▣ At one side of the crystal you can now perceive a staircase that winds up towards the uppermost regions of the crystal. Begin to climb the staircase, breathing in the energy, seeing the sparks of orgone as you climb. Notice how the energy is more intense at this level. At the top of the staircase you become aware of a platform upon which is seated the elemental who dwells within the crystal. Remember that you have entered its home without invitation, so project love and pink light towards the platform.

▣ Take note of its appearance. It might appear to be a bright spot of energy, or an angel, or a pixie, dwarf, or elf. It will appear to you in a form that you can understand; if someone else visits the same elemental, that person might see something entirely different. Understand that it is communicating to you on a basic level information about its personality and energies. Await as it responds to your thoughts of love. When you feel as though it accepts your right to be there, approach it. Advise the elemental of your requirements in the work that you are trying to accomplish, of your purpose in acquiring this crystal, and ask it how it will help you. Become familiar with the elemental, remaining open to whatever message it gives you. This message will always be presented in a spirit of love and joy.

▣ The spirit of the elemental is on that plane to learn and grow, so ask it how you can best help it in this growth. Your purpose is not only to take, but to give. Ask the elemental what it would like you to give.

▣ When you feel you have established some sort of rapport with the elemental, send it love and light, and then descend the crystal staircase until you are once again at the doorway where you entered. Color flows around you; take this opportunity once again to allow the colored energy to flow through you as you feel yourself becoming more energized. Leave the crystal through the same doorway by which you entered, and visualize it becoming very solid and impenetrable.

Crystals and Chakras

If you are reading an aura, the energy of chakras can be seen as colored light. The seven colors of the rainbow correspond to the colors emitted by the seven major chakras. Using these color correspondences, various crystals can be used in working with the chakras. The basic color of a crystal determines with which chakra it works best.

Here is a brief list of some color correspondences for working with crystals to energize the chakras. These crystals are readily available in a well-stocked store that sells crystals, and none of them are very expensive, since you are working with stones of less than gem quality.

Chakra	Color		Crystals
1. Base	Red	Garnet	Smoky Quartz
		Obsidian	Ruby
2. Navel	Orange	Tiger Eye	Red Citrine
		Carnelian	Sunstone
3. Solar Plexus	Yellow	Citrine	Turquoise
		Malachite	Topaz
		Beryl	
4. Heart	Green	Tourmaline (Green or Watermelon)	Aventurine Jade Bloodstone
		Rose Quartz	Malachite
		Emerald	
5. Throat	Blue	Sodalite	Lapis Lazuli
		Azurite	Clear Quartz
		Non-fire Opals	Aqua Aura
		Blue Quartz	Celestite
		Blue Topaz	Sapphire
		Blue Tourmaline	
6. Third Eye	Indigo	Lapis Lazuli	Sodalite
		Sapphire	Fluorite
		Sugilite	Dark Aquamarine
		Amethyst	Clear Quartz
7. Crown	Purple/ Violet	Lapis Lazuli	Celestite
		Fluorite	Amethyst
		Clear Quartz	Fire Opal
		Alexandrite	Fuschite

You might notice that some of the crystals in the correspondence chart above are of a different color than expected. For example, the color of the crown chakra corresponds with purple, but fuschite is a very delicate shade of green, fire opals are more red than anything else, and clear quartz has no color at all. The color correspondences are a *guide*, not a rule. You can generally use any purple or violet crystal to work with the crown chakra, and you will be successful. However, as the chart shows, other colors are equally effective. This list is comprised of my own experiences of many years. As you explore the crystalline realm, you will also find certain crystals that work well in various circumstances. That is part of the adventure of working with crystals.

Use the chart as a starting point. The stones listed are some with which I have had success. As you work with other crystals, feel free to add them to this list.

It is also helpful to keep a crystal journal or notebook. While you might be ecstatic today about the discovery that a certain crystal is helpful for a certain purpose, it is likely that in five years time, if you have not used the crystal for that purpose, you will have forgotten your discovery.

16

Ethics

Regardless of the metaphysical area in which you decide to work, there are a few universal principles that apply. Many people have some negative perceptions of those who work with the psychic realms, and historically, this has been for good reason. Traditionally, the field of metaphysics has been filled with crooks and idiots... or at least they always had the most press! Those who worked positively through their higher selves have always been out there, but kept a much lower profile and, therefore, got less publicity.

Be aware that even if you choose not to subscribe to any particular code of ethics, your higher self does. In metaphysics, this is called *working from the vibration*. You are a representation of your higher self on the physical plane, and whatever you do here is a reflection of what your higher self is working on in the higher realms. If your higher self has worked on a topic before and has learned something from that work, it will not allow you to undo that effort. If you work against your own higher-self energy, the end results will have little value or will actually work against you.

Here are some of the ethics that I subscribe to. I have always applied them. I have seen the results in the lives of others when they tried to work around them: total chaos.

There is not much growth in chaos because you cannot focus.

I can only advise you to read them over and to see if they seem appropriate for your life and your situation. You cannot just say that you subscribe to them. You have to believe that this is the only way that things will work for you. This is not a complete list; feel free to add others that work for you.

Manipulative actions never work - and they will rebound on the sender. After more than two decades studying and practicing, I can honestly say I have never known the cosmos not to return a valuable and well deserved lesson to anyone who thinks he or she can work manipulatively and get away with it. I am sure that, in a larger sense, a great deal of negative karma is invoked every time a person works to gain at another's expense, but in this area, "instant karma" is also often invoked. It is called **instant karma** because the moment you send out the manipulative action energetically, it instantly rebounds and the energy thus used begins working towards returning a lesson to you in your current lifetime. You will see the results of this kind of karma when something that you wanted for yourself does not happen.

Any attempt to use metaphysical means to attract someone with whom you think you are in love is considered manipulative. I have *never* seen this type of manipulation succeed for any length of time. Instead, direct all of this energy toward yourself. If you sincerely want to improve yourself, and you use your energy for this purpose, the energy will be drawn into your own aura. This in itself is an attractive force, and you will find someone compatible drawn to you because of the person you have become.

Do not meddle. I would venture to say that everyone has been advised at one time or another not to meddle in the lives of others. My grandmother used to say "sweep your own doorstep first." I think her advice is very wise! Metaphysically you cannot fix in another what is wrong in you, and paradoxically these are the areas to which we are all drawn. Our higher selves point out defects in ourselves by making them obvious in others. But, it is important to realize that the other person's higher self has incorporated this "personality defect" that you have identified for a good reason. Allow that person the space to have the "defect" and to learn to work with it. To that person, it is not a defect. Remember that "you don't know *best* because you don't know *all*."

The moment you find yourself wanting to cure the world's problems or the problems of another person, stop everything. Sit down and meditate. Refocus all of that energy towards yourself. Ask your guide or higher self about what is going on. Be aware that a genuine communication from either source will identify an area in *your* life that you need to work on, and they will help you refocus your energies in that direction. If you believe you are getting information that urges you to continue to deal with the world at large or with someone else's problems, it is not an accurately guided message and something is seriously blocked. Stop working until the blockage clears. Otherwise, you will find yourself in some situation that forces that change of direction and focus! Your guides always channel information meant for you before attempting to send information meant for others, so any information that appears not to apply to your own life is immediately suspect.

The path another takes is always right for him or her. Give people space! Each person's path is different. And, to point out the obvious: it is none of your business. Your concern is with your own path. Allow others - especially those you love - the space to make mistakes and do things with which you do not agree. What others do is their own concern. They have to deal with the results of their actions.

Yes, sometimes those results affect you too, but in those cases, you are actively learning something along with them. The results you see would not have occurred in those situations if the outcome was not helpful to you too!

Work positively. You can literally change your life by working positively. The same thing happens if you work negatively, but the reason most people send out negative energy is because some aspect of their life is not working at present. Unfortunately, what is not working out well now is going to work out even less when all that negative energy finds its way home! By doing the best you can, always, you are ensured good results. You are only required to be honest about what you do. Thinking that you can direct another's life, even a child's life, because you know better what might be good for them is totally dishonest (and incredibly overbearing!), and therefore negative. That person won't be affected by the energy you send out - you will.

One method that might prove helpful is to tell yourself before beginning any metaphysical work that your intent is to work for the good of all and to harm none. And then, do just that. Meditate carefully before beginning anything in the metaphysical area to determine exactly what is going on. It is helpful to use an affirmation to remind yourself before you begin *any* and *all* metaphysical work that your goal is to achieve the best results for everyone concerned. Remember, the karma that results from your actions will be directed into *your* life. It is far easier to ensure that your motives are positive before beginning anything than it is to try and rectify the results of inappropriate work after the fact.

It does not matter if it works or not. Whatever you do metaphysically must occur in accordance with universal principles. Forcing change is never appropriate, whether in your own life or someone else's. If it does not work then it was not supposed to work. This is governed from a higher plane. Since you cannot work around it, accept it. This principle applies frequently in psychic healing work when the person appears not to be responding. You cannot override the decisions made by the higher selves of others. Attempting to do that is useless and misdirects a great deal of your energy.

Learn to release. Energy is movement. Energy withheld cannot be effective. Nothing you do metaphysically will have any effect whatsoever if you "hold on" to the situation by, among other things, insisting on a certain outcome, insisting on being right about something, insisting that you know best, and so forth. While you are busily mentally gnawing on the situation, your energy flounders and dies, and nothing happens as a result. You absolutely *must* learn to release the outcome to the universe after you work with energy. This applies not only to psychic healing, but also to all other kinds of metaphysical activities.

Do not withhold positive information; always discard negative information. The same principle applies to withholding, or editing, information that you receive psychically. If not expressed, energy stops flowing. Never change what you receive. Changing the information only makes it less correct!

The only exception to this is the rare occasion that you receive information that someone will die soon, or have an accident, or that sort of thing. Feeling strongly that you are correct is insignificant. The universe is chock full of positive energies. That means that you can access any amount of good news just because you choose to. If the information you receive is negative, you can believe that it is not because your guides or your higher self wanted that to happen. Some negative energy inside yourself is pulling that information in. Once again, stop immediately. **Never** tell someone anything negative. There is no moral excuse for doing so, and it is extremely unethical. Do not change the information; simply affirm that you received it (say "yes" mentally) and then move on to your next impression. Remember, a reading is nothing more than your perception filtered through your own life experiences and there is no guarantee in place to ensure that your perceptions are 100% right. No matter what people tell you, they really do not want to hear any bad news.

Ethics for Psychic Healing

Developing your abilities as a psychic healer requires intense dedication and an incredible amount of study. If you are drawn to this field, you probably already have the ethical background necessary to work effectively. However, some general principles follow. The amount of training and intuitive work that you do in your early days directly affects the effectiveness and validity of your results. Do not even start to deal with anyone else until your life is going well!

Do not touch. When you work psychically, you are working with energetic bodies. Because they are less dense, they exist outside the outer edges of the physical, extending out several inches or feet in all directions. To work with these bodies, you do not need to touch the physical. If you want to include a massage or therapeutic touch, make sure you tell the person that is what you want to do. As a beginner, either work physically or work psychically. Concentrate on one and do the best you can. Trying to combine the two dilutes the effectiveness of both. Also, psychic healing of the physical works well through clothing.

Do not diagnose illness. Doing so makes you liable to

be sued for medical malpractice. Since arithmetically you have more chance of being wrong than of being right, avoid tempting the odds!

Before any psychic healing, direct the person also to seek medical help. This requirement helps the person focus on taking some positive action to improve their physical health. Taking responsibility for one's own health is a required first step before any healing occurs. Any changes in physical health will come from the person's own energetic bodies, not from you. Each physical body heals itself. Remember that physical healing must occur first. After that, you can help the person improve any psychic disorder.

Make no promises for a physical healing. Whatever happens after you have worked with the person's energy happens according to the person's higher self's master plan for that life. You have no input into that plan whatsoever. You cannot heal - the person does it - so do not promise what you cannot deliver.

Do not specify any remedies - such as taking vitamins - that you think might help a physical condition. It does not matter that you had the same symptoms and that this treatment worked for you. The same symptom can represent a number of illnesses. What helped you might not help someone else, and while they are trying your treatment, they are also most likely delaying seeing a physician.

For legal reasons, **NEVER** give anyone the idea, either by direct statement or implication, that your psychic healing work will improve any physical condition from which they suffer. Although they might experience a change in their physical condition, it is illegal almost everywhere in the United States of America to make such a claim. Medical malpractice is a crime, regardless of whether or not you were paid for the work. Be aware that the penalties are severe.

Keep your ego out of it. Hippocrates, the father of modern medicine, warned physicians not to play God with their clients. He reminded them that healing happens within the body, not as a result of the physician's ministrations. If the person's health improves, great! If not, it is not your problem, nor your concern. You have not failed, you simply did not have to offer what the person needed. Allow the energy of the healing to occur and then release the entire affair to universal energies. Having to see the results you desire rather than what the person needs sets up some nasty karma! If you cannot stay emotionally detached, you will have very little effect.

Index

A

absentee healing 101
affirmations 81
akasha 71
akashic realm 71
akashic record. 71
alpha-wave 22
altered state of consciousness 22
angelic realm 82
arrangement of topics 5
assisted self-regression 87
astral body 38
astral cord 62
astral travel 60
astral travel in dreams exercise 63
astrology/horoscopes 124
aura cleansing 101
aura readings 55, 127
automatic writing 125

B

base chakra 44
basics 13
beta-wave 22
biorhythms 126
blocking 122
breathing 15
breathing color 101
breathing exercise 17

C

caring for crystals 142
care and feeding of thoughtforms 68
centering 16
chakra balancing 100
chakras 44
channelling 125, 131
channelling exercise - meeting your guide 134
channels 47
channels in the crown chakra 47, 49
charged water therapy 100
charging crystals 141
choosing crystals 140
clairaudience 128
clairsentience 129
clairvoyance 128
clearing crystals 141
collecting energy 16
color correspondences 146
color energies and chakras 108
color exercise 114
color for the imagination impaired 113
color therapy 100
conscious astral travel exercise 62
considerations for past life regressions 95
creating a thoughtform exercise 66
creative visualization 25
creative visualization exercise 28
crown chakra 46
crystal attunement exercise 139
crystal therapy 100
crystal visualization exercise 144
crystals 137
crystals and chakras 146

D

developing receptivity 40
dis-ease 98
discarnate being 131

disreputable psychics 119
dowsing 126
dream interpretation 124
dream journal 8
dwarves 144

E

editing the information 122
Einstein's Special Theory of Relativity 13
elementals 143
elves 144
energetic bodies and chakras 52
energizing the aura with color 113
entities 131
etheric body 37
ethics 149
ethics for psychic healing 154
exercises 6

F

fairies 144
fossil 71

G

generator crystals 142
getting started 5
gnomes 143
graphology 125
grounding 16
group study 9
guides 131

H

handwriting analysis 125
healing 97

heart chakra 45
higher self 77
horoscopes 124
how channelling works 133
how the tools work 128
hypnotic trance 132

I

I-ching 124
if your thoughtform does not work 69
imagination 25
incarnation 77
instant karma 150

K

karma 72
keeping journals 8
kingdoms 137
Kirlian photography 125

L

learning to see the aura 52
ley lines 126
lower astral entities 59, 131
lucid dreaming 124

M

manipulating your energy 39
medical malpractice 155
meditate 31
meditation visualization exercise 33
mediumship 127
memory 72
mental body 38
metaphysics 14
methods for psychic healing 100
methods for receiving psychic information 123
movement 137

N

navel chakra 45
numerology 125

O

open a chakra 49
Ouija board 132
over-soul 77

P

palmistry 125
past life reading 88
past life regression 77, 127
past life regression exercise 84
past lives 83
pendulum dowsing 126
performing a psychic reading 120
personal space 44
physical body 37
pixies 144
preliminary steps for all psychic work 15
projective state 6
projectively using crystals 142
protection 58
psychic drawing 127
psychic readings 115
psychic senses 128
psychometry 124

Q

quantum 14

R

rainbow 107
realm 82
receiving a psychic reading 115
receptive state 6

receptively using crystals 142
regressing to a significant past life exercise 92
reincarnation 77
relaxation 19
relaxation exercise 23
relaxation techniques 20
relaxing 16
runes 124

S

salamanders 143
scanning a past life for details 94
scrying 127
seeing the aura 54
self-healing 98
self-regression 87
self-study 9
simple relaxation technique 23
sixth sense 128
solar plexus chakra 45
soul 37
soul groups 80
spirit guides, channeling 127
spiritual body 38
spiritual guides and soul groups 81
spiritual mediumship 131
sylphs 143

T

tarot card reading 124
tea leaves 127
techniques for past life regression 86
telepathy exercise 41
theory of quantum physics 14
third eye chakra 46
thoughtforms 65, 132
throat chakra 46
tools 98
trance channelling 125, 132

transcendental meditation 31

U

undines 143
using healing energy 101

V

vibrational levels 137
void, the 112

W

white light 21, 60, 108
working from the vibration 149
Working on the Astral Plane 64
Working With Color 107
Working with Color and Energy 110
Working With Crystals 140

Z

Zener cards 40

Order Form

Telephone Orders: Call 919-779-4620 between 10:00 AM and 4:00 PM Monday through Friday.

FAX Orders: 919-779-9508

Postal Orders: Three Pyramids Publishing, 201 Kenwood Meadows Drive, Raleigh, North Carolina 27603-8314 USA.

Please send the following books.

_____
_____
_____
_____

___ Please add my name to your mailing list.

Name: _____
Address: _____
City: _____
Telephone: _____

Sales Tax: Please add 6% for books shipped to a North Carolina address.

Shipping: $3.50 for the first book, and $1.00 for each additional book.

Order Form

Telephone Orders: Call 919-779-4620 between 10:00 AM and 4:00 PM Monday through Friday.

FAX Orders: 919-779-9508

Postal Orders: Three Pyramids Publishing, 201 Kenwood Meadows Drive, Raleigh, North Carolina 27603-8314 USA.

Please send the following books.

_____
_____
_____
_____

____ Please add my name to your mailing list.

Name: _____
Address: _____
City: _____
Telephone: _____

Sales Tax: Please add 6% for books shipped to a North Carolina address.

Shipping: $3.50 for the first book, and $1.00 for each additional book.